FROM
ONE CHILD
TO TWO

FROM ONE CHILD TO TWO

*What to expect, how to cope,
and how to enjoy your
growing family*

❧◉❧

Judy Dunn

FAWCETT COLUMBINE / NEW YORK

A Fawcett Columbine Book
Published by Ballantine Books

Library of Congress Catalog Card Number: 94-25563

ISBN: 0-449-90645-0

Cover design by Judy Herbstman

Cover photos (clockwise from top left) copyright © L. White/Westlight, copyright © Kim Robbie/The Stock Market, and copyright © Ariel Skelley/The Stock Market

Text design by Mary A. Wirth

Manufactured in the United States of America

10 9 8 7 6 5 4 3 2

Contents

FROM
ONE CHILD
TO TWO

Introduction

Some brothers and sisters get along well, others can't stand each other. Some are painfully jealous and competitive, some are interested and caring, and others feel a mixture of affection, irritation, and rivalry toward each other. Relationships vary strikingly between different sibling pairs. Whether our children like each other or quarrel endlessly matters tremendously to most of us. The relationship between siblings is, after all, the longest-lasting they'll have in their lifetime—longer than marriage, and longer than their relationships with us, their parents, or with their own children. Helping get that relationship off to a good start is a primary concern for most of us.

Before the birth of our second child, many of us worry about how our first child will cope with the changes in the family and about what we can do to cushion the blow. Our questions about the new family structure abound. What is the best way to provide help and support for a newly displaced firstborn? Is the age gap between the children important? How does gender affect the way that the children relate to each other? What kind of preparation for the arrival makes sense for a toddler? A preschooler? A five-year-old? How can I best introduce the new baby into my toddler's life? Should I plan for my older child to start daycare around the time of the birth? Will visiting in the hospital help my first child, or will it just add to the stress?

As the new baby grows up, the questions multiply: How can I cope with their jealousy and quarrels? If my first child shows signs of upset or unhappiness—stops sleeping or won't do a thing I ask her—does this mean the problems will persist? What's the best strategy to take in defusing aggression? Parents often feel helpless to deal with the intense competitiveness between their children. And they wonder why *some* young brothers and sisters get along so well while *theirs* quarrel endlessly. Or, if their children get on well in the first two years, they wonder whether the sunny relationship is likely to continue.

For the eighty percent of parents in the United States who have more than one child, these questions can loom very large. In this book, I try to answer these questions and many others like them in a direct and practical way, armed with the most recent research findings as well as with the comments of parents who are themselves coping with young children. As a psychologist with a special interest in children's social relationships, I have, for the last fifteen years, been studying young brothers and sisters—playing, fighting, comforting, teasing each other—and talking to their mothers and to the children themselves about their relationships. I've followed one group of brothers and sisters for more than ten years, meeting them first as toddlers and then revisiting them over the years until they were teenagers. In a separate study which began *before* the second child was born, we focused on the firstborn children as they coped with all the upheaval surrounding the siblings' arrival, then revisited the children repeatedly over the next two years. All my research is done in the children's own homes, so I've seen all the no-holds-barred battles and disagreements, *and* the affection and play that parents know so well. In the chapters that follow I'll draw on what we have learned from this research and from the spate of other recent studies on brothers and sisters to show you how to support your first child through a major change in his or her world, and how to foster happy relationships between your children. This is a book written for parents, and full of the voices of parents; but I back up all the assertions I make with my research findings, as well as the studies of my colleagues in the field.

Assumptions and myths abound about the way children react to the arrival of a brother or sister, and about why siblings do or don't get along—and many of these assumptions have been challenged by the new research. For instance, we have found considerable *differences* in how children react to the birth of a sibling and in how they relate to both older and younger siblings as the years go by. For you, as a parent, what's important here is that any general advice you receive is not likely to apply equally well to all your children, for the simple reason that your children are likely to be so varied in their personalities, reactions, and relationships. Advice that works for your easygoing, compliant, preschool son would not apply to your quicksilver, moody, toddler daughter. You have to take account of what *each of your* children is like in judging how relevant any advice may be. For each issue that we look at in this book, we'll discuss how children of different personalities are likely to react.

In most families the second child arrives when the firstborn is a toddler or preschooler, so I will look in particular detail at how children between eighteen months and four years of age cope with the changes and the new family member. In covering the first four years or so of the sibling relationship, I will show you what to expect in the way of their playing, fighting, affection, and antipathy for each other, their vying for your love and attention, and their joking together. Since more and more families are delaying the birth of a second child, I will discuss five- and six-year-olds too.

How can you help your child to weather the storms ahead?

How can you help *yourself* to meet both children's needs and wants? And how can you make sure *your* needs are met in the hurly-burly of raising two children (not to mention spouse, house, and job too). I know all too well about that hurly-burly, as I had three children under two years old: My twin boys arrived when my firstborn daughter was just eighteen months. Let's begin with the changes you'll face when you go from caring for one child to two.

PART ONE

The First Two Years

Chapter 1

CARING FOR TWO

It's just totally different now that there are two of them. I sometimes feel pulled in two completely opposite directions—I'm one kind of mom for Tom, and a quite different kind of mom for Kelly. They have such different needs, and they're such different kids. It's *hard*.

ANN, MOTHER OF TOM, 6, AND KELLY, 1

I feel satisfied—happy—now in a way I didn't before—tired of course, but more content—it's quite a change. The kids are in a kind of "honeymoon" period now when they're just great together. Just to see Josh's delight when Joy comes home, and to see her concern for him, and to hear them laughing together—well, it is just wonderful. I *love* having the two of them.

KAY, MOTHER OF JOY, 5, AND JOSH, 18 MONTHS

Although Ann and Kay had very different reactions to being mothers of two, they both stress the *change* that having a second child involves. Change is perhaps the only thing you can be certain of, both in what you feel and in the demands that you'll have to face. And with change comes a whole new set of worries and concerns: Are you doing something terrible to your firstborn by bringing a new star onto the scene? Will you be able to love two children at once? Will coping with two children instead of one place a greater strain on your marriage? How much more work will it be? Working mothers justifiably worry about how they'll cope with the demands of a full-time job as well as caring for two. This chapter addresses the fears and questions that naturally arise when parents are about to bring a second child into the family and during the early days of coping with two children for the first time.

CARING FOR TWO VERY DIFFERENT PEOPLE

Becoming a parent of two children means more than a return to diapers, interrupted nights, and attending to the needs of an infant. It means being the source of love, security, attention, and jokes, the finder of lost toys, and the comforter and the controller for *two very different people*. Lots of parents are bowled over by just *how* different their two children are. As Joy put it: "When I fantasized about number two I imagined him or her to be a carbon copy of my first . . . and that he or she'd fit rather neatly into the family. What a shock when she finally arrived and was so different! Instead of a calm, easy baby, she was forever restless and crying."

It can be quite surprising, even distressing, to realize that your second child is nothing like what you had imagined—especially if your first was an easy baby who slept through the night and number two is a cryer. Even with the distress, however, you may find that this experience draws on resources of love and caring you didn't know you had. Kath, mother of five-year-old Dan and his younger sister Jane, realized that she felt "a different kind of loving" for her quiet, somewhat withdrawn son and her cheerful, outgoing daughter. "I *worry* more about him," she confessed, "and we don't have so many jokes together."

Some parents worry that their very special, intense relationship with their first child is likely to take a knock from which it won't recover with the birth of number two, that it will be irrevocably changed. There will, of course, be changes in this special relationship as in all your family relationships; but this does not mean that you will love your first child less. In fact, many parents feel a heightened sensitivity to the firstborn's need for love and reassurance right after the birth of the second. This can actually strengthen their bond.

Some parents worry whether they will be able to love *two* children. How can you love another child when you adore the first one so? Once the second baby is on the scene, you'll find this isn't a problem. What you feel for each child will be different, however. The unspoken assumption often is that parents will—or should—love all their children equally all the time. But because brothers and sisters are so different from one another, and their particular needs and demands differ at any given time, isn't it unlikely that you'll feel exactly *the same* about each of them?

The answer is yes. Your commitment to each of your children can be equal and total, your love for each as intense, yet it is very likely there will be differences in how you relate to each of them. Most parents go through times when they're more concerned about or more attentive to one of their children than the others. This is only to be expected as particular problems occur or particular developmental issues take center stage. Most parents also find there are differences in the ways that they and their different children express their love for one another. Ray, a father of a five-year-old and a three-year-old, sees it this way: "One's a great cuddler—always on my knee—the other's close to me in a different way—we *do* things together and talk—but it's less physical."

Parents of twins are often particularly worried about this issue, and there is a lesson here for all parents. With twins, there are of-

ten phases when one or the other gets more attention and response from other family members. But things *do* tend to even
out over time. All parents of more than one child must deal with
the reality that giving one child what he needs at a given moment
often means a momentary neglect of the other. But, as with
twins, our children usually end up getting equal—if not identical—love and attention over time. Of course, if you notice that
the imbalance is continuing, then you may need to make an extra
effort for the child getting the short end. Remember that in the
end what really matters to your children is the *big* picture—and
the feeling that they are loved.

HAVE I RUINED MY FIRST CHILD'S LIFE?

Most parents' chief concern as they await the arrival of their second baby—and in the months that follow—is that their beloved
firstborn will be upset by the changes. However much a three-
year-old has said he wants a baby brother or sister, it's inevitable
that he'll feel displaced in some ways. But have you ruined his
life? The answer is no. The pleasures and strengths that siblings
give to each other as they grow up together are just as important
as the upsets and resentments. The *very great majority* of siblings—
whether first or later born, whether they fought endlessly as little
ones or not—say, both as older children and as adults, that they
are glad they have siblings, and that the relationship is important
to them. And the majority of only children say that they wished
they had had brothers and sisters, at least for some periods of their
lives. Strange as this may sound to you now as yet another battle
erupts between your children, siblings tend to look back with
affection and pleasure on the turmoil and fights, the companion-
ship and laughter, the shared experiences. Conflict between

brothers and sisters is absolutely *normal*, though it can be a real pain for you to live through.

Siblings relate to each other very differently from how they relate to their parents. They can "tune in" to each other as equals in a way their parents never really understand. There's a special pleasure in playing and joking with a sibling—and, different as they may be, they often share excitements and amusements. They can learn a lot from each other, though it's not through "teaching." And they can support each other in times of stress or upset. Many brothers and sisters give that support astonishingly early.

So try not to feel *guilty* about what you have done to your firstborn. And don't worry that your second born is going to be a deprived child because you can't give him the exclusive attention and adoration that your first child enjoyed. Of course parental guilt is as natural as sibling fighting, but it really is unnecessary and in any case not helpful to anyone.

CHANGES THAT PARENTS GO THROUGH

Having a second child may give you a new sense of perspective about being a parent. With a second you worry less about what's normal, and you worry less that problems are *your fault*. For many parents, caring for a newborn just seems *easier* the second time around, regardless of their differences in temperament. As one father put it, "You don't fuss so much about what's the *usual*, the *normal* things kids do, the second time. You *know* when they're tired, you *know* that problems pass. And although I have less time for each of them, in a way that has its positive side—I think I'm more relaxed with each of them, not hovering over them."

A sunny, easygoing second child often means a much easier "meshing" between child and parent than with the firstborn. Parents who had been ambivalent about having their first child and who found the first year or two of their first child's life a strain often relax into enjoying their second's babyhood much more.

Don't, however, count on your second being an easier baby—or you may be disappointed. The only thing you can count on is that there'll be differences between them. June's firstborn daughter, Karen, had been an easy baby, so she found it was rough when Ally turned out to be lively and restless all day and all night. "With Karen I used to think those parents who moaned about their crying kids and sleepless nights just didn't cope well," she says. "But now *I'm* at my wits' end." Having a more difficult child second has undermined some of June's confidence in her parenting skills.

Even when your second born sleeps and feeds like an angel, the escalating demands of a baby and an older child can lead to new heights of tiredness and irritation, and you may find yourself slipping dramatically from your ideal of calm and reasoned parenthood. Many parents with a firstborn preschooler or toddler and a second baby discover a new side of themselves, one they don't always like. June felt disturbed when she became quite a different mother to four-year-old Karen after restless Ally arrived on the scene. "I felt I was a really good mother with Karen. I wouldn't call myself that now. I'm irritable, tired, I don't do all those nice things with her anymore."

Lauren, mother of three-year-old Cheryl and six-month-old Stacey, had a similar story:

> I'm really upset that I can't *manage* Cheryl anymore now. It's a blow to my self-esteem that I don't know how to get her to behave. I used to find reading books to her at bedtime a wonderful, close time with her—now it's a nightmare. She's

always saying, "You skipped." "Read one more." "You read that wrong." Then I am definitely *not* the patient, calm Mom I used to be. A lot of it is because I feel pulled in two directions.

When a toddler launches an attack on a new baby, even a mother who has never spanked and rarely raises her voice to her firstborn is likely to explode with anger, and she may very well raise her hand. When you have a hungry baby crying to be fed, and a difficult preschooler who is obstinately thwarting that effort, you may end up resorting to bribes of chocolate even if you disapprove of candy between meals. If you disapprove of letting preschoolers watch videos or TV, wait until you are desperate for a quiet moment with your second child. Your practices and rules may well shift a good deal in the first months after the second baby arrives.

If you have become used to coping calmly with temper tantrums at the store, to changing the diapers of a bucking bronco, to cooking and eating with one hand while you draw entertaining pictures with the other, or explaining gently for the umpteenth time why that plastic duck can't really go swimming in the simmering soup, then you may feel that you have parenthood down pat. But just wait until your toddler piles his toys on the baby's face, or stuffs his blanket into her mouth. What parent could possibly be as patient and good-humored as she was before? To make matters worse, your older child may very well pick up on your guilt feelings and exploit them to her own advantage. "Why have you ruined my life?" was the devastating question asked by one articulate four-year-old when his mother brought his baby brother home from the hospital. Is there *any* answer to such a question?

If you feel you're always failing to be the parent you'd like to be, remember that *no one* is that perfect parent. The heartening thing is that children are tremendously resilient to parents' inconsistencies, lapses in patience, or occasional bad moods. What matters to them is the general day-to-day level of love and security they feel—not your occasional mood swings.

Expect changes in how you feel about housework and immaculately run households too. "Until you have two children, you think your carpets really matter!" one mother wryly observed. You can expect a shift in your priorities—and some differences in your views from those of friends with only one child! Don't be disheartened by their different standards—just wait till they too have two!

TWO CHILDREN DOES NOT MEAN TWICE THE WORK

After the second child arrives, the family workload goes up dramatically. Having two or more kids is *hard physical labor*, especially in the early months and especially if your firstborn is three or under when the new baby comes. There are the feedings, the diaper changing, the laundry, the errands to run, the picking up of a tired toddler, the complex logistics of just getting the two of them ready to go out, the running battles, and the running noses. Then, when you finally have a moment to yourself, forget those plans for a quiet cup of coffee because the baby has just thrown up, is crying, or needs feeding *again*. When there are two parents and one child, the work can be shared, but when it is two on two, your chances to sit down and take a break recede very fast indeed.

But take heart: After the first few months parents very often report that even though having two young children means a lot more noise, a lot less time to yourself, and a lot more work, it doesn't multiply by two. Time spent on meals, laundry, getting ready for outings, entertaining the little ones, doesn't double—it's more like a job and a half according to many parents. You often get into a routine more quickly with your second, for instance, and are experienced at finding those "shortcuts" in housework and baby care. Of course, some parents, especially those who have a big gap between their children, find that having two can be like having twenty, at least initially. But eventually most parents settle into routines and surprise even themselves with how well they manage their expanded family.

YOUR MARRIAGE: NEW TENSIONS AND NEW STRENGTHS

With all the upheaval and new emotions of adding a second child, many parents find that their own relationship changes too. You and your spouse are both often exhausted in those early weeks, and with levels of irritation escalating, you may find yourselves angrily accusing each other of not doing a fair share of the work. It is often when fathers don't pitch in to help during this stressful time that marital strains begin to tell. You may also disagree testily about how best to handle a difficult firstborn child (give in to all those new demands because he's upset and jealous? try to keep the old "rules" constant?), or a crying, inconsolable baby (put him out of earshot? cuddle him because he's in distress?). Fathers sometimes feel even more pressure to provide for the family, and that leads to longer working hours. And, needless to say, the two of you have even less time available for each other. Your sex life can suffer—even temporarily disappear—and that of course adds to tension. Many parents say that taking time out together—dinners out, movies—is crucial after the second baby arrives, though it becomes harder to make the arrangements.

But there is often a bright side too. First, mothers and fathers often draw closer through coping together (or struggling to cope together); this is especially true when both parents wanted the second child.

A second—and very big plus—is that another child often increases the father's involvement with his family. With two children to love and care for, the father is less likely to feel excluded from that intense mother-child bond. Fathers in single-child families commonly feel like the odd man out. They never really have a chance to get close to the child, and their relationship with their wife suffers too. Mothers can be so totally wrapped up in their love affair with their new baby that they simply don't notice. Or the situation is reversed: There is an intense father-firstborn attachment, and it's the mother who feels left out. Either way, the arrival of the second child often means a change to a happier family pattern. As Donna, mother of Beth and three-year-old Keith, remarked:

> We're a much more balanced family having two kids than we ever were having one. Maybe I wouldn't have said that right away after Keith was born, but it's certainly true now. When we just had one, Beth really just liked only me. She didn't like to spend much time with her dad, and he was very upset about it. But the second baby forced a lot of changes—it resulted in a realignment, which was in the long run so much better for all of us.

FATHERS AND FIRSTBORNS

The tie between fathers and their older children often strengthens when mothers are away in the hospital or busy with the new baby. It's a good time for many fathers and their oldest, a time when they become closer. Dad may take over bathtime and bedtime rituals somewhat reluctantly at first, but he frequently comes to value his new responsibilities. As one father of two commented: "Since the baby came, I've found myself doing much more at the bathing and bedtime with our oldest. I always felt uncomfortable doing it before and didn't really enjoy it— especially when he yelled that he wanted his mom. It's odd, but we *both* get a kick out of it now!"

The more a father is involved with his children early on, the greater his pleasure in both kids as the months go by, the closer his relationships with the children later on—and, of course, the less exhausted his spouse. Fathers of twins, for example, who tend out of necessity to be more actively involved in their babies' care, are often closer to their children than fathers of singletons. As one father with his four-year-old on his back and his one-year-old clambering up his legs put it, "It took having *two* kids to make me a father!"

TIMING AND SPACING: MYTHS AND REALITIES

Whether your second baby is actually on the way or you are still contemplating having a second, you have probably thought a lot about the optimal spacing between the older and younger child. Is a gap of one year better than two, or is it better to wait three or more years? There is no simple universal answer to this question. How you choose to space your children obviously depends on a host of personal matters—your and your spouse's work situations, your finances, your health and energy, your age, your personal preferences. You may want a longish gap between the children so you can regain strength before starting in again on diapers and sleepless nights, or you may want to get the diaper stage over as quickly as possible. Some enthusiastic first-time parents just want plenty of time to get to know and enjoy their first before bringing a new one on the scene. You've probably heard lots of conflicting stories about the impact of the age gap on sibling relations: There are those who insist that close-in-age children are more rivalrous, that two years is the "worst" gap *or*, alternatively, that they'll be better companions if they are close in age. What do we actually *know* about the consequences of different age gaps between siblings?

As far as your children's intellectual development or health goes, the age gap between siblings doesn't turn out to be important. Both intellectual development and health in children are influenced by a wide range of factors, from heredity to the quality of schools they attend. The same goes for differences in personality, in spite of what you may have heard about "the middle-child syndrome" or the "neurotic, adult-oriented firstborn." Neither birth order nor the spacing between siblings is the key influence on personality and adjustment. More important are temperamental differences among children and their relationships with the others in their world.

What about the relationship between the children themselves? Obviously how young brothers and sisters play together and the things they argue over is affected by their ages. But the age gap between them does not predict whether they'll feel affectionate or hostile toward each other. Children who are very close in age *and* those who are widely spaced can get along very well. But they can also dislike each other and argue a lot or ignore each other. Much more important in how they'll get along is the difference in their personalities—some children are compatible from day one; others just rub each other the wrong way—and the way each child gets along with his or her parents. A key factor is whether one child feels unloved or loved less than the other, or unfairly treated by the parents.

This does not mean that the timing of siblings has *no* impact on the pattern of relationships within the family but rather that it is one factor among many. Clearly, there is no "right" or "wrong" interval. Every pattern of timing has its own advantages and disadvantages. Here are some to consider:

Less Than Two Years

Parents who space their children close together cite these advantages: Getting over the baby stage quickly; making sure the siblings will be companions for each other, since they'll be at similar developmental levels and may well share interests and always have another kid to play with; your own age—many mothers who are in their mid- or late-thirties feel that if they are going to have more than one they had better get on with it!

Most parents who have brought up closely spaced children are glad they did it—once they have lived through the first few years! It is undeniably *very* hard work in the first two years. Be prepared for months of double diaper duty, of carrying *two* little ones upstairs at once, of juggling two nap schedules. Your ability to entertain your restless toddler while feeding your hungry baby will become very well developed over the next few months. Your toddler's amazing ingenuity at causing havoc with the baby's bath water or dirty diapers means you'll probably become adept at telling toddler-age jokes and doing song-and-dance routines as distractions. Dealing with two children under three can be a real trial for parents as a couple when the demands on each of them are so high.

Children of *any* age can feel jealousy and distress at the changes in their lives, but toddlers express these emotions quite differently from older children. Children who are between twelve and twenty-four months are likely to cling and cry a good deal and sometimes lose their ability to play in a focused way; older toddlers will often give up on newfound toilet skills, refuse food, and may start waking often at night, or become difficult to settle at naptime. Toddlers often don't have the emotional resources to cope with their overwhelming feelings, but simply go under— and that distress and anger can be hard for everyone. In Chapters Three and Four I discuss these different signs of upset and jealousy along with the ways parents can help toddlers through their troubles.

Two to Four Years

This is the most common spacing, and very many families end up with a three-year-old and a new baby. If your firstborn is only just two, many of the practical problems of the spacing will still loom large. A two-year-old firstborn still needs lots of help, yet he's also bursting with independence—an explosive mixture as you try to feed and care for the new baby.

The practical advantages of a spacing of three to four years are most apparent in the early months. With a three- to four-year-old the worst of the night waking is likely to be over, and toilet training established. Your older child is likely to be able to dress himself and feed himself, a blessing for you.

Older two-year-olds and three- and four-year-olds, however, often take their feelings out on their poor mothers: They become particularly demanding, contrary, and difficult. At preschool they may start behaving like Attila the Hun toward the other children.

On the other hand, a three-year-old, particularly one in preschool, is quite likely to have friends of his own, which can be a real support for him and can give you more time to enjoy your baby in peace. A child who has a social world that matters to him outside the home won't find the transformation of the new baby's arrival quite so devastating. When he's jealous or unhappy, you can both talk about it.

If your firstborn is nearing four years old, don't expect him to be free of jealousy and distress. Remember that four-year-old who asked his mother "Why have you ruined my life?" when she brought his brother home from the hospital? Of course not all four-year-olds are this manipulative—or this upset about a sibling's birth. It just doesn't make much sense to generalize too broadly about how children are likely to react. When you see statements about the disadvantages of the two- to four-year age gap, judge them with some skepticism, and think about your *own* preschooler and what you know about his personality, his moods, his social skills, his relationship with you. These are going to be better predictors of how he'll react than the number of months between him and the baby.

Four Years or More

It is becoming increasingly common for parents to wait four or more years before having a second baby, and there are some clear advantages to doing it this way. Each child gets plenty of that special love and attention as a baby. Parents whose firstborn is four or five years old have more time to enjoy the baby, since their older child is usually well launched in a life outside the family and is often less likely to be very jealous—indeed she may be quite interested in and close to the baby. The first year or so is undoubtedly calmer with this age gap. Of course your five-year-old may be *both* jealous and interested, but at least you and he can articulate some of his feelings and resentment.

Your sophisticated four- or five-year-old can *tell* you if she feels upset, or puzzled, or excited about the baby—which is a huge help to you both. And she can understand so much more about what is happening in her family than a bewildered eighteen-month-old. You can explain to her why you are tired, and why the baby has to be fed *now*, and she will be better able to wait until you are free to do things with her. You can explain, too, how precious she is to you, you can join in her games and make-believe, you can talk about plans for fun together. By this age many children seem to be more in control of their own (previously explosive) feelings too. Jon noticed that his five-year-old found ways to calm himself down when he was upset. He would go off and play with his favorite toys, for example, or ask to watch a favorite video: "A year ago," said Jon, "we had to help him through his tantrums."

Siblings spaced four or more years apart are less likely to be playmates than those who are closer in age—their interests are simply too different. They may well be friendly—in fact, as your second born grows up, they often *talk* together more than those who are close in age—but at a fundamental level they are independent from each other. But even with the remoteness, competition can still erupt, as we'll discuss in Chapters Eight and Nine. Siblings who are four or more years older than the next child are often put in charge as caregivers, and this, too, can be a source of resentment. On the other hand, older siblings can derive great pleasure from looking after the baby and they can be amazingly helpful and competent. You'll have to judge how much she enjoys it, and try not to "use" her if she's getting resentful. Often a much younger sibling feels a real hero-worship for the firstborn, and the older child can be quite proud of "his" younger brother or sister—and proud of himself for being the family "hero."

If you are concerned about how to choose when to have your next one, the bottom line is *not to worry*. There is no right answer, and we now know that the number of months between siblings is not the key issue it was once thought to be. You should do what feels right for you and your family. Your own feelings about it and how you see the needs of your family should be your guides. Every gap has its pluses and minuses. Remember that whatever you decide, there will be some advantages.

Chapter 2

YOUR SECOND PREGNANCY

When you're pregnant for the second time, you probably remember pretty well from your first experience the symptoms, sensations, and the changes to expect. You're an old hand. But there will also be plenty of differences from that first pregnancy and birth—differences in how you feel about being pregnant, and how everyone around you feels about it (don't expect to be cherished and cosseted this time), as well as differences in your physical symptoms, and in the actual birth. That very special excitement, awe, and joy of so many first pregnancies may well be missing; for many parents the moment of learning about the first pregnancy is etched indelibly on their minds but they cannot even recall what they felt when they learned about the second pregnancy. Those who do recall the moment generally speak of happiness rather than ecstasy. But worries, anxieties, and fears during this pregnancy are usually far fewer too. If all went well with the first baby, there's usually much less worry about the baby growing inside, although some older mothers who've waited several years for their second find that they feel *more* anxious and concerned about the course of pregnancy this time. Having amniocentesis or a medical problem you didn't have the first time can be a potent source of worry.

Most of us also feel less worried about how we will cope as parents the second time around. "Will I be *able* to handle a newborn baby?" we wonder before the first child arrives. "*How* will I take care of him? What kind of a father or mother will I be?" We pretty much know the answers the second time. There's an especially big difference in your fears and worries about labor and delivery the second time. Mothers who had a reasonably easy first experience are usually confident that it will be repeated, while those who had a hard time frequently (and conveniently) forget much of the pain of a difficult first birth—until the second labor begins!

But the biggest difference between your two pregnancies is that your firstborn is now on the scene, needing your love, care, and attention. Sometimes he'll distract you from thinking about your pregnancy aches and pains and discomfort, sometimes his extra demands will feel like the straw that breaks this particular pregnant camel's back. The physical demands of dealing with a toddler's or preschooler's needs—finding that truck, getting that drink, changing that diaper when you are sick to your stomach and just plain exhausted—engenders a fatigue that goes way beyond the tiredness you felt when you were pregnant the first time. And, of course, you won't be able to nap whenever you feel like it, as you did with number one. Four- and five-year-olds can be pretty demanding too: They sometimes react to the pregnancy by becoming more dependent and needing extra attention from you.

More first-time-pregnant women remain at full-time jobs than those pregnant with their second child, yet as many women discover for themselves managing a full-time job outside the home plus a first-time pregnancy is usually *not* as exhausting as managing a second-time pregnancy, plus a young child, plus a part-time job.

So you should really *expect* to feel particularly exhausted this time. Unfortunately you're also likely to get much less help and pampering from your family and friends than you did with your first pregnancy. When you are pregnant with your second child you are usually expected to cope competently, very much on your own. There are differences even in how your obstetrician will care for you: Doctors looking after second-timers often focus more on the physical side of the pregnancy and less on the emotional aspects than they do with first-time-pregnant women. Most people, including doctors, seem to assume that second-timers can handle anxieties and fears during pregnancy much more easily than first-timers. This means that if you *do* have worries you may have to be more direct in asking for help. You may be able to get in touch with a support group of other pregnant mothers. Talking to others who are in the same boat may well provide the most help of all.

Don't be surprised if your body changes are different this time.

You may "show" much earlier than in your first pregnancy: The stretching of your abdominal muscles in the first pregnancy means a bigger bulge, earlier, this time. For the same reasons, you may carry the baby lower. Your breasts, however, may not become so large as the first time, nor feel as sore. Those great moments when you hear the heartbeat and feel the baby move for the first time may come earlier—in the fourth month rather than the fifth. It's not completely understood why this is so, but one theory is that the uterus wall stretches slightly thinner the second time so you can feel what's happening inside more easily.

As for the common complaints and discomforts of pregnancy, there is some good news and some bad news for second-timers. If during your first pregnancy you suffered from swelling of hands and feet, that painful accumulation of water in the tissues, you may do so again, but it's unlikely that the condition will be worse the second time around, at least if you don't gain too much weight. (Second-timers often don't keep to their diets or watch their weight gain as assiduously as first-timers. This *is* important and worth your attention—for the baby's sake as well as yours.) And you are unlikely to develop more stretch marks, again if you don't gain too much weight. On the other hand, varicose veins in the legs, and hemorrhoids are more likely to occur. If you have trouble with varicose veins, put up your feet, or better yet stay off them as much as possible. Varicose veins usually shrink back to their prepregnancy size after the baby is born, you'll be glad to hear. Discuss what to do about painful hemorrhoids with your doctor. Backache is often worse the second time around—probably because the joints are looser and don't hold you together so tightly. If you are troubled with back pain, a massage, a heating pad, even a well-fitted girdle, can provide some relief. Some doctors think these physical problems are more likely with very closely spaced births, and they recommend at least eighteen months between births for this reason.

If you have bouts of nausea in the early months, join the club: About one in two women suffers this way in early pregnancy. "Morning sickness" is more common in second pregnancies, so even if you didn't suffer from it in your first, you may get it now. Try small snacks of dry crackers or other dry foods at intervals during the day, beginning with a couple before you start the day. Heartburn, too, may strike for the first time in a second pregnancy, and if you had it in your first pregnancy, it may be worse this time. Again, ask your physician about how to get relief.

As far as the more serious complications of pregnancy go, preeclampsia is less likely during second, third, or later pregnancies, though high blood pressure may be more of a problem for older women due to the loss of elasticity of the blood vessels. Miscarriages are probably no more common in second than first pregnancies. Anemia may be more of a problem if the second pregnancy follows very soon after the first: Your body may not have had time to build up the stores of iron that are needed to replenish the supply of iron that is transferred to the fetus. A word of warning here about iron pills: Keep those pills well out of the way of your firstborn child. Too many children end up in the hospital because they have been trying out their mothers' iron pills.

BETTER NEWS: LABOR AND DELIVERY

The good news about second pregnancies is that your labor and delivery will probably be much easier than they were the first time. Don't, however, expect to know when labor is beginning any more clearly than you did the first time. In fact, that disconcerting "false labor" (when you have a few contractions well before labor starts in earnest) is *more* common in women who have already given birth. If it's been several years since your first child was born, you might want to take a refresher course in Lamaze. More second babies arrive on or near their due dates than do first babies, but the length of a second pregnancy has little connection with the timing of the first: Even if your first baby arrived very early, you have an excellent chance of a full-term baby next time around. Alternatively, if your first birth was induced, you won't necessarily be induced the second time, and vice versa.

It is the length of labor that is likely to be very different the second time. On average, second labors are only half as long as those seemingly endless first labors. Even though your contractions will be just as strong, knowing that the whole process will be over faster should make it easier to bear. And of course it helps that this time you know what to expect. A shorter labor is good for the baby too—less stressful on his system as well as yours. And that's especially true for the second stage of labor, when the baby is moving through the birth canal. While the second stage often lasts one to two hours in a first delivery, it usually lasts under an hour with a second delivery, and can be even shorter. Keep in mind, however, that individual experiences vary considerably. A shorter, easier second labor and delivery is the statistical norm— but there are exceptions.

Even more good news is that you may not need an episiotomy—that small cut in the perineum that's made just before the baby is born—even if you had one with your first baby. The stretching of the perineum from your first delivery means that it is more flexible; if you do need one, it may be a smaller cut than the first time. After the delivery, your milk will probably come in sooner than it did the first time, and getting your second baby going on breastfeeding is likely to be easier from the start, since you know how to go about it.

A CESAREAN BIRTH?

Whether you will have a cesarean section this time depends on the reason the cesarean was performed in your first delivery. If it was because you have a small pelvis—one of the common reasons for cesarean sections—then you'll probably have one again: You haven't, after all, become larger! If health reasons such as diabetes or a heart problem necessitated the first C-section, then that, too, will make it likely you'll have a cesarean again. But if your cesarean was related to a condition in your pregnancy that may not recur—your baby was distressed, for instance—then you may not have to have a C-section this time; it will depend on your obstetrician's views, in part, and you should discuss it with her or him in advance. And remember that cesarean sections do have their advantages—they often involve less anesthesia, for instance, than a normal delivery. You'll also know when you're going to the hospital, a distinct advantage when you have to make child-care arrangements for number one.

Chapter 3

PREPARING FOR THE ARRIVAL

What will this change be like for Joanne? Will she be upset when the baby first comes home? We keep wondering how we can help her. She's been the center of all our attention—how *will* she take this change?

SALLY, MOTHER OF 32-MONTH-OLD JOANNE

Joanne, a bouncy, outgoing nearly-three-year-old was the happy queen of her world before the arrival of sister Polly. Like lots of other parents, Joanne's mother Sally felt increasingly anxious as the end of the reign of the only child loomed. Would this be a major stress for Joanne? What could Sally do to cushion the blow?

There are no hard and fast answers to these questions—so much depends on the individual child and her parents. Various "experts" have taken a strong position of how to "prepare" a child for the birth of a sibling, some advocating lengthy discussions and lots of books, while others claim that it makes no difference. The fact is, there is no good hard evidence for either position. This is partly because almost all children get *some* preparation for the arrival. Even if no one has spent time reading stories about babies to them or explained in detail what will happen, they hear adults talk about the baby, and they've usually been around babies at one time or another. So we really have no basis for judging how a child would react to a baby without *any* preparation. And, since children's reactions vary so much depending on their ages and their family circumstances, we have no way to generalize.

But we do have some clues about what is likely to be important in preparing children for the arrival. These clues come from what research has revealed about children's reactions to changes and stressful events, and from studies of how siblings get along over the months that follow the arrival—and probably most important of all from what parents have said about their own children. But remember these are *clues*, not firmly established facts.

These clues suggest that preparation probably does not make a great deal of difference after the first few days. Preparation may affect that initial reaction to the new baby, but the first response can change from sunshine to storms after the first week or so. Take Arnold, for example, a three-year-old in one of our studies in England. Arnold had been well "prepared" for his sister's arrival with stories and conversation, and when he first met the new baby he seemed happy enough. "I gave him her to hold the moment I came in the door," recalls his mother. "He was delighted and cuddled her. He didn't want me to put her in the stroller. Just sat and held her."

But over the course of the next three weeks Arnold became

very angry and difficult, and then after a month he began to withdraw. "Now it seems as if he's in a world of his own," his mother said six weeks after the baby's arrival. "So quiet. I think he's feeling pushed out. When people come to visit, he used to get so excited. Now he's so quiet." Arnold in fact became quite sad and depressed over the next few months and did not bounce back.

The preparatory books and conversations about babies were clearly not all that helpful to Arnold. But keeping the whole topic hushed up or ignoring his questions would probably have been a worse approach. If your child is curious about what is going to happen, or is seeking reassurance about the baby, or shows a lot of interest in babies, then I believe it is important to talk to him about the baby and to discuss what will be happening when the baby comes. Trying to minimize your child's potential upset through preparation is, after all, an act of love and reaching out that at some level he'll feel and understand.

If you do want to try to prepare your child for the impending changes in his life, here are some guidelines:

TALKING TOGETHER ABOUT THE NEW BABY

How much and what kind of preparation will suit your child depends largely on her personality type and age. The "preparation" you can give your engaging but not yet verbal eighteen-month-old is obviously very different from the preparation you'd plan for a sophisticated six-year-old. When considering *when* to tell the child about the pregnancy, keep in mind that very young children have a different sense of time from our own. A child under three who is told about the baby early in pregnancy may become bored with the whole business well before the baby actually comes. It makes sense to take your cues from your child. Your toddler, two- or three-year-old may begin to ask questions about your new shape at this time, and these questions make a good opening to talk about the baby.

As for *what* to tell him, keep it simple: Your toddler doesn't need a lecture on reproduction. You could say, "We're going to have a new baby in the family. The baby is growing inside me, from a very tiny egg." Then wait to see if he has any questions. If you tell him the baby's growing inside you, tell him it's *his* baby sister or brother that's growing there. And explain that this is how *he* grew inside you, that when the baby is big enough, you will go to the hospital and the baby will be born—just as *he* was born.

If you get questions like "Can I see the baby?" "Was I in there too?" keep your answers simple, short, and truthful—and expect more questions! "We can't see the baby till he's born, but you can feel him move—put your hand there and you'll feel him!" "Yes, you were in there, you grew in there just as this baby is growing." It is a very difficult concept for a preschool child to get hold of, so beware of overloading your little one with too much informa- tion. (But no storks—even if your child loves *Dumbo*!)

As for telling him *when* the baby will be born, if your first child is a young preschooler, you can connect the timing to something that has meaning for him: "The baby will come in the winter around Christmastime." "The baby will arrive around Halloween."

Children also differ in how much they *want* to hear about a new baby brother or sister, and especially in how much they worry about the impending event. Some children are just not that interested. Some are curious, but not "motherly," while other children *love* babies and want to hear more. Still others tend to worry, and for these it doesn't help at all to harp on all the changes that the new arrival will bring. Jamie, an anxious three-year-old boy, asked twenty times a day about his soon-to-be-born baby sibling; his mother wisely began to introduce other topics. If you have a firstborn who is anxious, like Jamie, remember, too, that this is a time when extra reassurance of love and support will be very welcome.

Four-year-old Andy was both fascinated with and puzzled by the idea of the baby growing inside his mother and by what would happen at the birth, and he wanted to sort out his confusions. Repeated conversations with his father and mother clearly helped him, and he gradually began to picture the baby as a person. If you have a curious four-, five-, or six-year-old, by all means discuss it with him. You'll probably have some great conversations about the baby. But keep an ear open for signs that the questions are in fact motivated by a need for reassurance—not solely disinterested, scientific curiosity. Your child may want reassurance that he is still going to be loved, or he may be worried about his possessions, his room, his world being invaded. A six-year-old can be very responsible and grown-up, but he still needs extra affection at times of change. After all, he has reigned supreme and had his parents to himself for six whole years.

TALK ABOUT THE BABY AS A PERSON

Conversations with your first child about what the baby will be like and how he will be able to help you with the baby can affirm his sense of himself as a helpful, capable person. Let him feel the baby move inside you. That's often an exciting moment for first-born children, and one that helps them to understand that the baby is a person and not just a bulge in your tummy. If the baby gets hiccups, let him feel that too—it makes the baby more real to him. If you know the sex of your second baby already, then you can talk about your firstborn's *brother* or *sister*—again, it will help to demystify the business. Explain that the baby will be small and likely to cry quite a bit—at least at first.

Children five and older can grasp the idea of the baby growing and developing quite well. Your child may be interested in pictures showing the growth of the baby through the various stages of gestation.

TALK ABOUT YOUR FIRSTBORN'S BIRTH

Most children have an insatiable appetite for stories about themselves, and it can be a real help to talk to them about what happened in their *own* growth and birth, and then relate that to the baby kicking inside. Sharing these stories so they become a familiar "ritual" can be a happy experience for you both. Focus on whatever details you can remember of her birth and infancy. Show her photos of yourself pregnant with her, and then at the hospital after her birth and of herself in her hospital outfit. One father reports that his son's favorite video at this time was one they'd made of *him* as a baby.

READ BOOKS TOGETHER

Reading books about a second baby coming can be a help. One mother advises: "Get one that shows the new baby crying, not just pictures of babies being all sweetness and light! They find out that's not true all too soon!" If you can find a book about a child who has *your* child's name, that's an extra bonus. The benefits of these books are that they make the oncoming event more real, and they help your firstborn to understand how his life will change.

Another activity that can be really fun is to work together on a book about your first child's arrival and early months. You can gear it to his age and to what he can understand—for instance if you have a four-year-old who is curious about the baby growing inside you, you could include a drawing of yourself with *him* inside. One mother unearthed some photos showing the whole progression from hospital, to first feeding, to going home, meeting the grandparents for the first time, and so on. "My son and I stuck them in this little book," she says. "It was fun for both of us! And he used to ask to 'read' it at bedtime."

ASK FOR HIS IDEAS ABOUT A NAME

Let your firstborn help to choose names for the second. If he comes up with an absurdity, it could always be the family nickname for his brother or sister—or *his* own special name for the baby.

EXPLAIN WHY YOU ARE TIRED

If you are exhausted because of the pregnancy, tell your child why so she doesn't feel it's because you are ill (which might worry her), or because you don't want her or aren't interested in her. And by all means continue cuddling your firstborn: That phrase "I can't lift you up because of the baby" *won't* help your toddler feel good about the impending arrival. Lift until you really can't do it anymore and then don't say that you can't—just try to do lots of cuddling while you are sitting or lying down.

AVOID MYSTERIES OR ANXIETIES

Even a child under age two picks up when you are talking about the baby with other people. So it makes sense not to be secretive or mysterious about the baby. Mystery may cause worry. Talk to your firstborn about where she will stay while you are in the hospital in a matter-of-fact way. Explain that after the baby arrives you'll still go on doing all the things you do together now—the walks, special games, bedtime routines. Two-year-old Jane asked repeatedly if the baby would sleep in *her* crib, clearly curious but also definitely anxious about giving up her crib. Her parents reassured her that the baby would have its own cradle at first and she could keep her crib.

Older children are also often concerned about what will happen to their favorite possessions after the baby comes. "Will the baby play with my *toys*?" asked one five-year-old again and again, obviously wanting reassurance. If your firstborn is anxious about this, give him reassurance clearly and patiently that his toys won't be commandeered by the newborn baby—even if the proposition seems ridiculous to you. Possessions can matter so much to two- and three-year-olds—we should respect that significance. Their toys are part of the all-important architecture of their daily life, and the fear that such items may be taken by an intruder can shake a child deeply.

It's a good idea to keep any worries you yourself may have about the pregnancy or the baby well under wraps; keep the conversations comfortable and calm. Remember, too, that a newborn can be pretty disappointing for your child. One mother promised her son a brother who would play soccer with him—and of course the "real" baby was very far from the soccer star her son expected. Similarly, visitors or relatives who say "You're going to have a lovely sister to play with" should be firmly overridden— she's simply not going to have that playmate for several months.

PROVIDE CONTACT WITH BABIES

Children who have received a lot of preparation sometimes develop very specific expectations about what the baby will be like, and then feel very let down by the reality. Lauren took her three-year-old daughter Cheryl to a preparatory class in which the children played with dolls and pretended the doll was their new baby brother or sister. But the enterprise backfired. As Lauren now recalls with chagrin: "She had her own version of everything so she could do it all, beforehand, with her baby doll. She had the stories, saw the hospital, everything. Well, I suppose it might have been even worse if we hadn't done all that, but it still didn't make the first weeks easy! Cheryl loved baby dolls, and it was a great disappointment that the baby wasn't a baby doll. She was way too heavy, she cried too much—so the *real* baby was a terrible disappointment to her. It was really the letdown—her *expectations* that made things difficult."

Having more contact with a real baby might have helped Cheryl. Another preschool child saw an engaging, cheerful ten-month-old who visited his school one day, and he used that single encounter as the basis for his image of his new sister. He was very disappointed with his "own" new baby sibling when she appeared—crying, red-faced, and wrinkled. It is worth the effort, then, to try to *have infants around if possible*: Seeing actual newborn babies helps children of any age get a sense of what to expect. Try baby-sitting for a friend with a new baby and take your own along so he can see you with a baby; if you have a friend who is breastfeeding, let him watch so that it will seem less strange when *you* do it.

Some parents find that having a pet can also help. It's a distraction, something to love, something that is fragile and needs protection. One child watched the family cat give birth and learned from this how fragile and vulnerable a baby kitten is. His mother helped him relate all this to the baby-to-come.

However carefully you have prepared your firstborn, you may find that he's still upset, angry, or overwhelmed by the reality of the new baby. But when you stop to think it's really not surprising that preparation seems to fly out the window in the face of reality—when reality means your mother can't pick you up and cuddle you because of the baby, that she's tired and upset, and that your daily life is turned upside down. Think about how you as an adult can be rationally "prepared" for something that's going to happen (the birth of your first baby, separation from a friend, or the death of a loved one), yet you're still devastated when it happens. Then think how much more devastated your toddler or preschooler will feel when the new baby changes his home life forever. The bottom line is that preparation won't hurt, and it may provide some enjoyable new activities for you and your firstborn to share before the baby arrives—but don't expect it to work miracles.

MINIMIZING CHANGES

The upset that follows a sibling's birth is undoubtedly greater for children who have to cope with lots of changes in their daily life at the time of the baby's arrival. So the most helpful ways that you can prepare your firstborn baby—whatever his or her age—is by keeping those changes to a minimum. One change you can't avoid is that someone other than you will be caring for him while you're in the hospital.

OTHER-THAN-MOTHER CARE

Firstborn children who have gotten used to separation from their mothers *before* the sibling comes (for instance, those who go to daycare, or whose mothers work) are usually less upset by the upheaval of events surrounding the arrival of the baby than those for whom it is a first-time major separation. So it is a good idea to get your child used to your being away for brief periods, and to having someone other than you look after him before the baby's birth. Best of all, of course, is to have the person who will be taking care of him when you are in the hospital come occasionally, or regularly, well before you have to be away. A child who is used to daycare or preschool and who enjoys going may find this continuing, stable, unchanging setting a real source of support at a time when his family life is suddenly a bit chaotic and daily routine seems to have disappeared! For some children, going to school every day can make them feel excluded. If your child begs not to go, you can consider making alternative arrangements. But on the whole it is better to keep your child's routine as "ordinary" and predictable as possible over this period.

The last few months of pregnancy can also be a good time for fathers and mothers to begin taking turns over bedtime, bathtime, and dressing, taking to and picking up from the baby-sitter's, daycare, or school if those are jobs that Mom usually does. Then both child *and* father will be comfortable with these routines when Mom isn't there, or is busy after the baby comes. "Dad's way" of organizing bedtime, or getting supper ready may be different from Mom's, and it's great if your child is used to it *beforehand*—toddlers especially may get upset by changes in routine. Of course, some mothers find it hard to sit by and watch their husbands bumble through routines that they themselves have so smoothly under control. As Jayline said of the times when her husband is in charge: "When her dad looks after her you wouldn't believe the mess I have to deal with afterward—the place is chaos and she has the weirdest clothes on! I often think it's not worth it—leaving him in charge!"

But it *is* worth it—for both their sakes and yours. Just try to remember it *doesn't matter* if her dad doesn't do it all smoothly or "right"—if he puts the wrong clothes on, doesn't clean up, gets paint on the floor, or makes a mess in the bathroom. It is *not* important if the socks don't match, or that she's given food that she's not had before. What *does* matter is that both she and her dad have a good time together and get used to each other's ways. The same goes for grandmothers, aunts, and friends or other caregivers. It may be hard to hold back your comments on how things should be done—but hold them back anyway! Help is going to be so precious after the arrival—do everything you can now to make the potential helpers confident and comfortable.

"THAT'S MY CRIB!"

Many children become very upset when "their" crib is given to the new baby. So if you are planning to move your child from crib to big bed, it's a good idea to do this quite a while before the birth. You can make the new bed a *special treat*, a sign that she's an especially grown-up girl. It's probably best to take the crib apart and keep it apart till it is needed rather than simply move it to the baby's room or corner. If your child is still using her crib, this may not be the best time to move her into a bed, unless she is clearly ready and willing. Better to borrow a crib from a friend for the new one, or use a portable crib for a bit. Your new baby won't be fussy: He'll be perfectly happy in a basket or even a drawer for a while. If there is only a year between your two children, you might have to invest in a second crib.

Getting ready for the baby—buying clothes, moving furniture around, preparing a crib—can be exciting for your child, or upsetting. If he is interested and wants to shop with you and plan, that's great—do it together. It may help minimize his sense of being left out if he has shared in the expeditions. But lots of young children find shopping exhausting and boring, so don't overdo it. You may find that you and your firstborn have very different ideas about which crib or stroller to get, and you may feel tempted to go along with your four-year-old's preference for wild pink bunnies and teddy bears all over everything to keep her happy. But remember she won't dislike the baby *less* just because he's asleep in the crib she herself picked out. If you don't want to get into a tussle, leave her home or at any rate don't put her in the position of choosing. You may also hear a lot of "*I* want a baby bath" "That's not the baby's, that's mine!" "*I* want my baby bed again!" When this happens, it's best to tread carefully. Try not to let the preparations dominate too much of your child's day, and don't overdo the "presents" for the expected baby.

TOILET TRAINING

If your first is not yet toilet trained, now is not the best moment to launch the campaign, even if the thought of two children in diapers seems overwhelming. If he really seems ready, you can try gently to see if he gets the hang of it, but as a general rule, it is better to wait at least a couple of months after the new baby arrives. When he's between two and three years old he'll probably pick it up very fast anyway, with a minimum of effort on your part.

DAYCARE OR PRESCHOOL

Now is not the time to enroll a child in daycare or preschool for the first time. Parents who have done so often look back on it as a mistake. As Kate realized with Roy: "We started him at preschool the week I came home from the hospital. At the time, I had no help and my husband had to go back to work, so it seemed the best thing. Roy didn't settle in at all and we had to give up on that plan."

It stands to reason that children sent to daycare for the first time just after their rival sibling has invaded their home would interpret it as a pointed rejection—and, in a way, they're right.

Similarly, removing a child from daycare can be a problem, as another parent noted: "Taking her out of daycare when the baby came was a mistake. We thought she'd want to be at home with me and the baby, so we took her out a couple of weeks before the baby came. But she missed her friends, and the structure of the day."

MOVING

Very often, having two children requires a family to move into a larger house or apartment. This change, of course, is one that you can't always control, but there is little doubt that these upheavals can add to the stress and disturbance in many toddlers and preschoolers—and even in older children. As Alex commented:

"It wasn't exactly a mistake, because we had no choice, but we moved the week my wife went to the hospital for the birth, and our daughter got very clingy and easily upset in the new house. I think it added to the strain for her *and* for us."

If you do have to move, the earlier in the pregnancy you do it, the better.

KEEP ON CUDDLING

If your firstborn is a toddler who likes to be carried a lot, and if lifting her is very hard for you, you can start doing lots of cuddling while you're sitting down. If she gets used to your sitting on the floor to cuddle and comfort her now, she won't be so disconcerted when you *can't* always pick her up after the new baby comes. Very gently steer your firstborn toward some more independence, encouraging her to walk up stairs (while you stay close behind), showing her how to put on some of her clothes, and praising her for performing simple tasks around the house. If he's old enough, you can teach him to climb into the tub from a low box or platform. Until he's steady, kneel down and hold his hands. But be very patient, and don't push for independence if it seems what he needs is extra *babying*.

EXPLAIN WHAT WILL HAPPEN
WHEN YOU GO TO THE HOSPITAL

As the date for your second baby's birth gets near, explain to your firstborn what will happen when you are in the hospital. Clearly and simply tell him where he will be staying, who will be looking after him, that his daily routine will be the same as it is now. Explain that you will talk to him on the phone from the hospital, and that he will come and see you in the hospital, and what that will be like. And, of course, most important of all, tell him you will come back home to him in a few days—often just a day or two. Don't dwell on the impending separation if it is making him anxious; just describe very calmly what will happen, then find something else that will interest him.

You can buy a present—ahead of time—for him to have in the hospital if you want. If you have a five- or six-year-old who likes food and cooking, you can prepare some special meals together to freeze, and he can share them with his dad while you are in the hospital.

SUMMARY OF TIPS

- *Talk about what your firstborn was like as a baby.*
  Focus on your firstborn as a baby, show her pictures or videos of her as a baby, and how she grew.
- *Talk about the baby as a person.*
  Let her feel the baby move and help you think up names. All this will make her feel more grown-up and capable, and begin to see the baby as a person.
- *Look at books together.*
  Read books together about what's going to happen.
- *Make a book about your firstborn's birth together.*
  Make an age-appropriate book that tells the story of your first child's arrival and early months; add drawings of you with him inside, and photos.
- *Have babies around.*
  Seeing real-life babies gives children a sense of what to expect. Baby-sit for friends, visit someone who is breastfeeding.
- *Pets can help.*

Pets are a distraction and something to love, and seeing how vulnerable baby animals are may help when the baby is there.

• *Keep on cuddling.*
Give him as much cuddling as he needs—sitting down if that's easier on your back.

• *Encourage helpers to start now!*
Encourage Dad, and grandparents if they're able and willing, to be part of the routine daily pattern of looking after your first. Don't wait until after the event to get new caretakers involved.

• *Explain clearly what will happen to him.*
Explain where he'll be when you're away, and who will look after him, and tell him about the hospital visits.

The final message: These are just ideas about how to help, not rules. Rather than fuss over preparation, enjoy your child *now*, and think about his current interests and the things you like doing together. Take more time off work before the birth, and have as much relaxed time with her as you can. Enjoy your last few weeks of being just the two of you. That's probably more important than trying to anticipate how she *might* react when the big event happens.

Chapter 4

AT THE HOSPITAL

When you are in the hospital your child will do best if the pattern of his daily life at home stays as near as possible to normal. Our study shows that children who have to cope with major changes in their daily routine as well as having no mom around experience more difficulties with the arrival of a sibling. This is especially true for toddlers and young preschoolers, but it's just as important for an older child who is anxious about changes in his routine—those kids who ask ten times a day where Mommy is, when Daddy is coming home, where they will stay when you go to the hospital, and so on. Some children get thrown even by seemingly small deviations, for example, if Grandmother forgets that they like to watch Sesame Street right after breakfast or that they need their special blanket to go to sleep with. So it is best if whoever is in charge when you are in the hospital knows the daily routine well. Tell the caregiver about his special likes and dislikes. If you can, get someone he knows and loves—a favorite grandmother is ideal, or his trusted baby-sitter.

Other kids flourish with or without their routines—and they remember for months afterward with huge delight all the strange new things they did while their mom was away. They recall these days not as a major trauma but as the time Daddy let me play with clay on the carpet, let me stay up late watching TV, lost my jacket, or the time I stayed with my best friend all night. If you have this kind of child, special treats and privileges could be a good thing to offer while you are away.

If you can't have anyone staying in the house with her, arrange to have her stay with a friend. This can work especially well with a child older than three. Three-year-old Sarah, who had never had a night away from her mother, went to stay with a daycare friend for one night when her brother was born, and it was a huge success. She talked and talked about it afterward, and asked if she could go and stay there again sometime. As always, you are in the best position to judge what will be the best and most practical arrangement for all of you, and to judge how your own child would react to the different kinds of arrangements that are possible.

PHONE CALLS FROM THE HOSPITAL

It's a good idea to telephone your eldest child from the hospital, and, if your stay is prolonged, to call at a regular, predictable time. But be prepared for some surprises in the response! Three-year-old Gordon was very excited about the idea of having a *brother*, and talked endlessly through his mother's pregnancy about this new baby *brother* and what they would do together. It was pure wishful thinking on his part, as his parents did not know the gender of the expected baby. Right after the baby's birth, his mother called Gordon to tell him the news:

> MOTHER: Gordon, we have happy news!
> You have a baby sister!
>
> [long pause]
>
> GORDON: Just what I wanted!

From that moment, Gordon never mentioned that he'd longed for a brother, and a delightfully warm relationship developed between him and his sister over time. Other parents have had a tougher time with that first phone call home. When Gordon's friend, Erin, was told over the telephone that her new brother would be coming home the next day, Erin replied: "We'll see about that!" If your firstborn is disappointed about the gender of the new sibling, don't agonize over it. And don't worry about silence or baby talk at the other end. Over the next few years the way they get along together is not going to be linked to this *initial* reaction.

THE FIRST MEETING BETWEEN THE SIBLINGS

Lots of mothers puzzle over how best to arrange that first meeting between the two siblings. Is it better to have them meet in the hospital or at home? Should he come home from daycare to find the baby right there in the center of things, or would it be best to make sure the baby was out of sight initially? These questions can loom large when your first child seems utterly indifferent to the baby. This was the case with Ray, a three-year-old in one of our studies. "He just wasn't interested in looking at her," his mother said with concern, "and got quite angry when we tried to get him interested. I began to think we should have 'introduced' them in some other way. Did it make it worse to have had them meet in the hospital?"

The fact is, Ray's mother need *not* have worried. Siblings are going to spend their whole childhood together—and how this very first meeting goes does not tell us how well they'll get along in the future. There is no "right way" or "wrong way" to arrange the first encounter.

TO VISIT OR NOT TO VISIT?

A prolonged battle raged in the United States in the last decades over whether to allow children to visit their mothers and siblings in the hospital. But when a few hospitals began to allow brothers and sisters in a few years back, the dam broke. Parents started basing their choice of hospitals partly on their policy over children visiting. And so hospital administrators, worried about losing revenue if they didn't welcome two-year-olds, relaxed the rules. Now siblings are permitted to visit just about everywhere. There are still big differences in how *eager* hospitals are to welcome your two-, three- and four-year-olds, and even your five- and six-year-olds, but it is now more a question of how often they'll let your children come rather than whether they will let them in at all.

On average, children who do *not* visit their mothers in the hospital are slightly more likely to ignore their mothers when they return home, and to refuse to hug and kiss them, than the children who do visit—at least when their mothers have had to stay several days in the hospital. Some behave this way because they're angry, others seem more depressed or anxious. And the great majority of children who visit their mothers in the hospital react positively to the hospital visit. Those children who have negative reactions are, in their mothers' words, "upset with wheelchairs," "overpowered by other visitors," "clingy," "upset." Reactions to seeing the baby in the hospital are quite often mixed: Many firstborns are simply not particularly interested or friendly toward the baby.

Some hospitals give you a choice of keeping the newborn in your room with you or leaving her in the nursery to be brought in for extended visits outside of visiting hours. As far as a firstborn child is concerned, it makes very little difference whether he sees his new sibling through the nursery glass in the company of a lot of other babies or alone with you in your hospital room. Chances are he'll feel pretty much the same toward the baby either way.

The big plus of the hospital visits is that it eases your child's anxiety about being separated from you, and vice versa. It is often very hard to be away from your first child; you will miss him as much as he misses you.

SHOULD YOUR FIRSTBORN BE
PRESENT AT THE BIRTH?

The practice of allowing older siblings to be present during delivery began in California in the late 1970s, and now a number of hospitals and maternity centers around the country have adopted this policy. Some restrict it to over fours, others to over twos. Those in favor believe that if children are present at the birth they will be more likely to feel lovingly attached to the new baby and will not suffer from the separation from their parents at this critical family event. This sounds logical enough, but there is no hard evidence for it.

If you think it is a bad idea, there are plenty of doctors and psychologists who agree with you! Although the intent may be loving, I personally feel this is *not* kind to children under five, or even to many older children. Children who have attended births show a wide range of reactions. Some are frightened by the overwhelming experience, by the blood, and the sight of their mother in pain. Other children are rather bored (one child said afterward he would rather have watched TV), while still others become highly involved and enjoy timing contractions. Quite aside from the children's reactions, many professionals feel it is not helpful for mothers if they are worrying about their older child while they give birth. Given the difficulty that under-sixes would have in comprehending what is happening to their mothers *and* the extra stress on mothers, my own view is that the firstborn child should *not* be present for his sibling's birth.

If, despite it all, you are still thinking seriously about having your firstborn present when the second is born, bear in mind these issues:

First, how old is the child? Most hospitals do not encourage parents to have children under four present. It is obviously harder to explain what is going on to a two-year-old than it is to a five-year-old—and to reassure him that his mom is really all right.

Second, how do you think *you* will react? Will you be able to relax with your child there?

Third, what does your firstborn really want? Some parents pressure (rather subtly) their firstborn to attend, even if the child is hesitant and a bit scared.

Fourth, make sure that you and your spouse agree about this.

If you decide on having your firstborn present, preparation classes available in the hospital for your child will be important. Also, take along books, snacks, and games to distract your firstborn during the slow moments. If your child shows any signs of wanting to leave, make sure she can do so right away.

Prepare Your Firstborn Ahead of Time

If you didn't talk about the hospital visits with your firstborn before you went to the hospital, have someone explain to him, gently, what he can expect before he arrives on the ward. Make sure he knows that you and he can cuddle and hug, that he will be able to see but probably not to touch the baby, and that you will be staying in the hospital when he leaves.

Several parents comment that it was a mistake to have the child brought to the hospital by his or her father, *but taken home by someone else* while the father stayed with the mother for a longer visit. So, if possible, make sure Dad takes him home, unless it is a special treat for him to go off with his grandparents or friends.

THE HOSPITAL VISITS

Don't Expect Too Much

Some children have fun in the hospital, like the three-year-old who wanted to round up all the cribs of the babies in the nursery to form a circle of "wagons" to keep out any (imaginary) Indians who might be threatening. Others find it all too much to take. Still others sit silent throughout the visit taking no notice of their poor mother (who is devastated as a result), or the baby.

"It was hard on Carla," said Sheila of her three-year-old. "I was in the hospital for four days with a C-section. It was really tough on her—she'd only been away from me one night. She had a fine time staying with friends, but the hospital visits were too much. The only hours that the hospital would let siblings visit was between seven and eight P.M., and she was so tired by then—she got too excited—she needed to be in bed by then. The visits were overwhelming for her."

If your child seems restless, tired, or upset during the visits, keep them short, and perhaps infrequent. Monitor how she is feeling and acting, and have your husband take her home before she falls apart.

Difficult Behavior at Home

Joan, mother of two-year-old Rob, describes an all-too-common worry for a mother marooned in the hospital:

> When they brought Rob, my first one, in at visiting time, they kept telling me how he was waking all night, wouldn't eat, and oh, it worried me. I thought I'd upset him for life!

But *don't* worry too much if your firstborn shows signs of upset like excessive crying or clinging or going back to wanting a bottle while you are in the hospital. I'd recommend allowing a certain amount of regression at home over these issues if it helps him over this rocky patch. These problems are very common during the separation, and almost certainly won't last long. They are signs that your eldest misses you and that he needs extra love and reassurance and attention. In most cases they don't last very long.

Be Prepared for Rejection Yourself!

If your older child seems angry or ignores you when she comes to visit, don't let it upset you too much. It does *not* mean she doesn't love you—any more than your disappearance to the hospital means that you don't love her—which is how some firstborn children interpret it! It's dreadful for you, of course, when you get stony silence, or when she glowers at you and clings to Dad. But it'll pass, and it is *common*. It does not foreshadow any long-term reaction.

Try Not to Have Too Many Visitors

A crowd means he won't have all your attention, and he may suffer even more if your visitors ignore him and coo over the baby instead. And all the bustle may be upsetting to a toddler or a young preschooler. Jack felt that it was a real mistake having too many visitors in the hospital when his two-year-old daughter Sue came. "We were all so excited and busy talking, she didn't really get a look at the baby. And then she was being all weird and difficult, so it ended up with her in tears. Instead of it being a happy time, it was a disaster!"

GIVE YOUR FIRSTBORN A PRESENT

Having a little present in the hospital for your firstborn is often a good idea. He may cling to it for dear life or he may decide to give it to the baby. Either way, it can cheer up someone who is just on the edge of being upset. Even seven- and eight-year-olds are pleased when the new baby's arrival means a little present for them too—and they often remember for several years what they got at this dramatic time. But avoid telling your firstborn that the present is *from* the baby, in the hope that this will increase his enthusiasm. He may really believe that box of Legos or that doll was *brought by the baby*, and this can be confusing, especially if you had previously told him that the baby was growing inside you. How on earth did this tiny, crying creature *bring* something for him? The present is a way of making him feel special and can be a connection with *you* that stays with your toddler or preschooler when he has to leave you and go home.

These days, most moms go home with their babies just a couple of days after the birth, and in some cases even sooner. You and your firstborn will find that things can change quite fast in the first weeks home, and that's what we look at next.

SUMMARY OF TIPS

- *Keep visits short and sweet.*
  Watch how your first child takes the hospital visit, and send him home if he becomes tired, restless, or worried.
- *Try not to have too many visitors.*
  They overwhelm him and mean he doesn't get your attention, which is what he needs.

- *Don't worry if you hear he's stopped sleeping or demands a bottle while you're away.*
  It's common, and it doesn't mean he won't enjoy his sibling, and it probably won't last long.
- *Be prepared for being rejected and ignored when he visits.*
- *Have a little present ready when he visits.*
- *Don't worry if he isn't interested in the baby.*
  This doesn't tell you anything about how they'll get along as the weeks go by.

Chapter 5

COMING HOME: LIFE WITH TWO IN THE FIRST THREE WEEKS

He asks where she is first thing every morning. He's happy when he can see her, and wants to cuddle and talk to her ... he's *sweet* to her—but oh, is he difficult with me!

KRIS, MOTHER OF THREE-YEAR-OLD IAN AND NEWBORN JO

Kris arrived home from the hospital, tired but eager to see her firstborn son Ian and anxious about his reaction. For Ian, the homecoming scene was enormously exciting: Here was his mom at last, after a long two days and nights away, and here was the baby he had heard so much talk about. Dad and Grandma, who'd been looking after him during the hospital stay, were there too. As Ian took in the new scene, his excitement escalated. He rushed in circles around everyone, wanting to hold the baby and pat her, demanding that Mom pick *him* up too, insisting that his dad play with his Legos with him, then immediately wanting Mom to read him a story. Kris handed baby Jo over to Dad and sat down, exhausted, to read to Ian—who promptly pushed her aside and wailed that it was his *dad* he wanted. When Kris left the room, he cried that he wanted her back, and howled when his grandmother tried to help.

And so the first week home continued. Ian was interested in Jo and seemed concerned when she cried. He wanted to help with washing her. But his demands on his mother, his whining, and his contrariness reached new heights. He seemed to find it difficult to play on his own, yet when Kris sat down to play with him, he sometimes just burst into tears for no apparent reason. Baby Jo was waking a lot at night, and breastfeeding was not going too well for Kris; when Ian started refusing to settle to sleep and began visiting his parents' bedroom several times in the night, Kris felt she had come to the end of her tether.

For almost all parents, and especially for mothers, these first weeks at home are sure to be difficult. Even if you're blessed with a placid and easy new baby, he will inevitably need lots of attention at all hours. You will be tired and sleep-deprived; your firstborn is likely to be upset and difficult. What's more, many mothers feel a combination of *irritation* at the endless demands and contrariness of their older child, and *guilt* that they've caused this unhappiness. Both feelings are very understandable, but neither helps you to stay calm amid the chaos.

Most firstborns feel supplanted in the first weeks as parental attention goes into a nosedive after the sibling appears. From the older child's point of view, not only do you get less time playing games with your parents, sitting on the floor, building, or reading books, but you also feel that your mother has lost her magical ability to catch your eye whenever you look at her or to notice and comment on your great achievements. And it's not just because she's with the wretched new baby: the change is evident *even when the baby is out of the way*. Mothers are tired and stressed and *busy*; when the new baby is finally asleep and fed, they often just want to collapse, or do some of the housework that is waiting to be done, or talk to their friends on the phone about the upheaval in their life. Kelly felt her three-year-old Tim had become more depressed, more quiet, and more touchy after the baby came home. She knew that part of the bad mood stemmed from her inability to give him the attention she used to. "Now he tends to get into the 'come and stop me' behaviors," she notes. "I try not to let it escalate, but often it does."

Margaret, five-year-old Ella's mother, faced a similar situation:

> I know I'm not doing things with Ella the way I used to,
> it's hard when I'm just so busy. There's just so much work,
> and my husband's away such long hours, I'm all alone. But
> I know I should try and make more time for her. We just
> don't get those quiet times together anymore, it seems. It's
> hard on Ella.

Children who suffer a particularly marked drop in parental attention are likely to be the most upset after the birth. So it is important to try to compensate in any way you can. Make the most of the time when the baby is sleeping to read books with your eldest; see if you can pick her up from school *without* the baby whenever possible. Give up on the housework for a while; get your husband to do the grocery shopping (even if it means getting it done late at night). The trouble that Margaret was having with Ella (that mixture of contrariness and demands that is so common) decreased noticeably when she managed to carve out an hour or two when she did things with Ella *on her own.*

So, however tired you are, however desperate for a bit of time away from anyone under five, it's worth taking extra trouble to do things with your eldest, to read books together, and to make sure there's lots of cuddling. Take her out alone if you can, even if it is just to mail letters or walk around the block. Watch that movie you both like, in bed together. It can work wonders.

HOW PARENTS REACT TO THE CHANGE

Your firstborn probably will not be the only one who is upset and bewildered by the changes in his family relationships. *You too* may find yourself missing that closeness you had with him before. Many mothers feel cut off from their firstborn child when they first come home from the hospital. They are tired and weak from the birth, busy with the new baby, and may feel preoccupied with trying to get breastfeeding established. Suddenly, on top of all this, their beloved first child seems to be a remote figure. Tina, mother of twenty-month-old Evan, described the feeling this way:

> It's like looking through frosted glass: I can *see* a blurred version of how we were together, so close, but I can't reach it, I can't get back to it.

This feeling of being cut off usually passes quite soon as you regain strength. But you may well feel nostalgic, every once in a while, for that closeness you shared with your first child before life was complicated with your second.

HOW FIRSTBORN CHILDREN
EXPRESS THEIR FEELINGS

Major changes in the structure of daily life are especially stressful for young children who can't control their emotions or understand what is happening to them. But insecurity about whether you are loved and jealousy of a usurper are powerful emotions at any age. Even five- and six-year-olds may need to be "babied" and reassured at this time. Supplanted firstborns express their reactions in different ways. Four-year-old Jeremy, whose mother had to stay in the hospital for several days because of complications following the birth, became withdrawn and quiet after she and his new brother came home. He sat for hours in the corner of the room, holding his teddy bear, or simply wandered around the house, unable to focus on his play. He didn't make demands on his mother, he was not interested at all in the baby. In contrast, twenty-three-month-old Kelly wanted to be carried and cuddled endlessly, and to have all the things the baby had. Jeremy's withdrawal, Kelly's escalating demands, and the whining and frantic contrariness of Ian (whom we met at the start of the chapter) are all expressions of powerful feelings and the need for reassurance.

Even if your firstborn's behavior is driving you to distraction, it's important to give her all the love and attention and cuddling you can spare now. That doesn't mean overindulging her or letting her break all the rules. It does mean trying to put yourself in her shoes and look at the world through her eyes. Keep in mind, however, that you may very well have problems with your eldest even with all the love and attention you can provide, and even though she's clearly enjoying the baby.

Let's take a closer look at some of the typical behaviors of oldest children in the first weeks after their mothers and new baby siblings come home. In most cases, these behaviors reflect their efforts to *cope* with overwhelming feelings beyond their control. Remember: These problems are *very common*, so don't feel they arise from your "failings" as a parent. And don't feel guilty.

DIFFICULTIES, DEMANDS, AND SETBACKS

Outrage, bewilderment, and just plain misery are common at this stage. You may have a child like Jeremy who withdraws into himself and just seems sad. Such withdrawal occurs in about 15 percent of firstborn children. Or you may have one who suddenly seems to have devilry in him that you never knew existed. Your sunny, equable three-year-old may appear to revert to a terrible two, far more terrible in fact than he ever was before.

Your child may suddenly need you all the time now. You can't go to the bathroom on your own, pop out to the store, or go down to the basement without those arms tight around your neck and that huge preschooler on your hip. Even if she's over two, she may now want to be carried upstairs to bed or the bath.

To add to your troubles, sleep disturbances are very common after the arrival home. The displaced firstborns are likely to wake up repeatedly in the night, to have trouble settling down to sleep, to appear like miniature Lady Macbeths in pajamas in the middle of your precious child-free evening moments. Two- or three-year-olds who have been toilet trained are quite likely to break down in their new accomplishment. In one of our studies, more than half the children who were toilet trained around the time of their sibling's birth had setbacks. Even four- and five-year-olds may lapse in their nighttime dryness. If your child loses her mastery, be as reassuring as you can, and as patient. Just lower your expectations for a while; she'll soon manage the toileting again.

If your child is a toddler, you are probably already experiencing struggles over meals: Expect more once the baby arrives. Again, patience and reassurance will help her to enjoy eating again.

The most common problem of all is an upsurge of "deliberate naughtiness." In these early weeks, very many children will repeatedly do *exactly* what they have been told not to do. In my research on young brothers and sisters, I have watched lots of children at home with their mothers and new siblings, and I've witnessed firstborn children again and again indulge in these previously forbidden activities. Wallpaper was systematically ripped from the wall, baby's bath was deliberately tipped over on the floor, the television the mother was watching was repeatedly switched off, a whole line of clean laundry was let down into the mud—the ingenuity of the actions was remarkable.

Especially interesting is the skill with which these toddlers and preschoolers pick the *one thing* that is most annoying to their parents. In our research we interviewed mothers in detail about their lives with their firstborn children, and we included questions about what the firstborn children did that they found especially irritating before the new baby came. Every mother had an example that came easily to mind: playing with the garbage pail in the kitchen; fiddling with the television channels the moment his mother sat down to watch; barging into the bathroom when his mother wanted a private moment. Preschoolers and even five- or six-year-olds had their own variations on these themes. What we found was that after the new baby arrived, there was a sudden escalation of *precisely* those actions that the mothers had particularly minded. In response, the firstborn always got attention, but most often it was irritation rather than reassurance.

How can you avoid this pattern? If you can identify these annoying actions, you can take preventive action (put the garbage pail in a closet, so he doesn't get the opportunity to play with it; make sure you get to put your feet up in front of the TV *while he's having a nap,* and so on). You can try extra hard to keep from showing your irritation this time, but it does require superhuman effort, which may well fail!

BOUTS OF JEALOUSY

This is a time when your firstborn may well be jealous of his dad's attention to the new baby, or of the grandparents' cooing over the new one. One child shocked her mother when she told her firmly, "Daddy is *not* Ronnie's daddy." It is quite common for firstborn children to show more signs of jealousy when their fathers play with or hold their new siblings than when their mothers do. As Laurie, mother of three-year-old Tammy commented:

> I think she takes me and him [baby] for granted. But she looks at her dad in a special way when he's with the baby.

Fathers often have a particularly exciting relationship with their young children, and it is very hard when *your* special daddy gets all absorbed in the baby. Sometimes fathers are so delighted by their new baby that they just don't notice how much their oldest cares. If this is happening in your family, point it out to him—it is after all a sign of how much his firstborn cares for him.

It may also be worth alerting your parents or parents-in-law to go easy in their enthusiastic attention to the baby if you notice it happening. Stress how close their oldest grandchild feels to them. But be sure to tell them about your first child's sensitivity out of her hearing: over the phone or when she's not within earshot.

HAPPIER MATTERS: THE FIRST SIGNS
OF THE SIBLING RELATIONSHIP

Four bright spots in these first weeks home: First, physical aggression to the baby is quite rare at this time. Although lots of older siblings deliberately provoke and irritate their new baby brothers or sisters—shaking the crib so the baby wakes, pulling the pacifier away from them, overwhelming them with noise and attention—they seldom inflict direct physical assault. Their rough behavior is often an expression of curiosity about this strange creature and how she reacts.

Second, the signs of disturbance in firstborn children are not usually linked to dislike of the baby. Far from it. Sometimes the children who are the most affectionate to and eager to care for and entertain the baby are the most difficult to live with in other ways.

A third positive sign is that some children show "great leaps forward" in independence at this time, suddenly insisting on dressing themselves or going to the toilet alone. It's wrong to think that children are only disturbed by the sibling's birth. Their response is often ambivalent—a combination of anger, distress, increasingly mature behavior, and genuine interest in and affection for the baby. They may feel upset and unsure that they're still loved, but at the same time they're friendly to the baby.

Fourth, your firstborn's friendliness to the baby is the beginning of the real relationship *between them* that you'll see growing in the next months. Children find their own way of relating to the baby, and it's touching to see. You may find, for instance, that your oldest loses interest in bathing and diapering the baby with you after the first couple of weeks (when he realizes that he can't actually do much of it himself); but as he discovers that the baby watches him, he begins to learn how to catch her attention, and starts his own "conversations" with her. As their relationship develops over the following weeks and months, the exchanges between them get more elaborate. We'll look in the next chapter at how you can support and help these "conversations," which can be so crucial to the developing relationship between them.

REGRESSION, COMFORT OBJECTS, AND OTHER COPING STRATEGIES

Regression into baby games and infant behaviors is common among firstborns at this time. Your firstborn may suddenly begin to play at being a baby animal—he is baby bear and his dad is Daddy Bear—or he may start squeaking and giving his version of baby noises. Or he may want you to pretend to change his make-believe diaper. Some children pretend to breastfeed or pretend that they are being breastfed. Such games often increase in the first month after the new baby arrives. One mother described how her two-year-old ran the gamut of regressive behaviors: "She wanted to try formula, she wanted to sleep in a crib. At first I thought, well, no, I won't stand for that, but then I thought oh, well, and let her, and she just tried each of them once and that was it, she found it wasn't so good." This mom was right in not being overly concerned about her daughter's regression. The baby play is just one way that children come to terms with the whole idea of babyhood and the fact of the baby. The feelings children are trying to cope with are complicated and powerful: "Playing" with the situation in a game that they are in charge of seems to be one potentially helpful way of sorting out these puzzling and overwhelming events. Regression is not a sign of trouble ahead.

Even a seemingly mature four- or five-year-old may indulge in some babyish behavior. It can be disconcerting for parents to watch a sophisticated kindergartner suddenly fall to pieces if she doesn't have her cuddly toy. This new—or resurging—passion for a soft toy, toy animal, blanket, or other "comfort object" is another way of coping with feelings of insecurity. Firstborns often suddenly begin to be more dependent on that comfort object, desperately wanting to have it with them at night, at daycare, at naptime, or when they're tired. Woe betide you if you go on a trip and forget to bring that special toy or blanket, or worse yet, take it with you on a trip and leave it behind in some motel. But don't get too concerned. This intense dependence on a crutch will pass in time. So give her that extra love and attention, "baby" her a bit, and talk to her about how *she* was a baby and how she gradually grew up to be your special three-year-old.

A third common coping strategy of older siblings is to ask lots of *questions*. Some three-, four-, and five-year-olds pose endless why, what, and how questions about the baby, about babies in general, about themselves as babies, about breastfeeding, bowel movements, babies' crying, and so on. They are not asking all these questions just to drive you crazy. Like adults, they want information to help them understand the stressful experiences they are going through. Your best approach is to try to answer these questions as simply—and as patiently—as you can manage, keeping in mind that all parents eventually reach the end of their fuse.

DEALING WITH THE CHANGES FOR YOUR FIRST CHILD

Even though it is reassuring to know how common these signs of mild upset are, it's still not easy to be the one taking the brunt of them. The following scenario is all too common: Not only do you have a newborn baby who needs feeding at all hours, who is unpredictable in that newborn way about sleep and routines, who needs immediate attention at odd times and often, and to whom you *want* to give attention. You also have to deal with another person—your firstborn—who knows exactly how to infuriate you, who refuses to sleep at night, and extends the bedtime rituals so it's a nightmare for you to get out of her room, who seems to have given up eating altogether, who whines, clings, and acts contrary. Who insists that you help her dress, then changes her mind and insists that it is Daddy she wants, then when you turn to deal with the baby, switches back to a wail for "Mommy dress me!"

So how do you survive all this *and* help your firstborn through a difficult transition? Here are some tips.

Remember the problems don't last long.

First, hang in there. Many of these signs of trouble last only three or four weeks, and most don't last beyond the first six months. For most children, the peak of extreme demands, of refusing to comply with your reasonable requests, or breakdown in toilet training passes in the first two to three months after the new baby comes home. Sleep difficulties may last a little longer, and you may well get a new surge of problems a little later on when the baby becomes mobile, but most children settle back into being happier and easier to live with in the next few months. It is a fairly safe bet that by nine months, the contrary and whining behavior will have ceased. However, if your child seems especially depressed and withdrawn or especially fearful and worried, this behavior may continue rather longer than the "acting out" reactions. Depression and anxiety are clear indications that your child needs extra attention and love. Though you might find it convenient when your first child lapses into quietly sucking her thumb every time the baby is fed or bathed or played with, don't ignore these behaviors. She may not respond to your usual overtures—you may have to make an extra effort to play and talk with her and to take her out on special activities—but by all means do it.

Problems now don't lead to fights later on.

It may help you to know that the children, especially the preschoolers, who give their mothers the most grief in this first phase often get along very well with their brothers and sisters as the little one grows up. They certainly get along *just as well* as the angelic older siblings who accept the new baby without a whimper. So don't despair. A firstborn's demands, naughtiness, and sleeping problems now does not mean that brother-sister quarrels are on the horizon.

Keep to a routine.

Younger children whose days change very markedly are more likely to show greater signs of upset than children whose routine remains constant. Your hospital stay itself was probably a major disruption for your firstborn. Now there's a stream of visitors who come and go, meals are strange and appear at odd times, no one takes her for walks anymore, her mother's too busy and tired to play. Things that seem trivial to an adult can loom large for a preschooler: drinking from a special cup, getting her favorite song at bedtime, or watching a certain TV show at a set time each day. When all these familiar habits cease at once, life begins to seem very uncertain to a young child.

So besides giving lots of attention to your first child, it's important to keep daily life as close as possible to what it used to be. You are the architect of your child's day, and you can make sure that the day is predictable and orderly. Keep naptimes and bedtimes constant; maintain bedtime routines like reading or storytelling. Remember regular outings like a walk or a trip to the grocery store. Make sure he continues to see his friends.

This adherence to the old familiar routine is less of an issue for most four- and five-year-olds than for younger children.

Make sure visitors are a help, not a problem.

"We managed pretty well when it was just me and the two of them," commented one mother. "But when visitors came—and they came all the time—or when her dad came home from work—that's when things just fell apart. She couldn't cope with all the upheaval, and was specially difficult."

Visitors may be a pleasure for you, but they are sometimes the last straw for a nearly hysterical toddler or preschooler. One mother, looking back ruefully, said, "I wish we had banned all visitors for a week and just settled down together."

If the visitors do come, you might remind them to pay some attention to your firstborn. And ask a few relatives to pick up a little present for big brother or sister in addition to their gifts for the baby. Even a small token can go a long way to minimize hurt feelings.

You will be the best judge of when your child is becoming overwhelmed by the stream of visitors. If your firstborn shows signs of upset over the visitors, or if you're having a hard time establishing harmony with your new family of four, don't hesitate to tell those visitors to wait a couple of weeks to see the new baby. You can also arrange for visitors to come when your older child is at preschool or school.

Let your oldest help with the baby.

Many friends, relatives, and neighbors and even some parenting books advise you to keep the baby out of the older child's life as much as possible. The prevailing theory is that a first child feels about as well disposed toward a new baby as you would feel if your husband brought home a new wife and expected the two of you to get along. Adherents to this theory tell you to avoid talking about the baby with the older child, to try to feed the baby away from the older one (how on earth that is to be achieved is not made clear), and so on.

But we now know from research that the opposite strategy—bringing the baby into the first child's life as much as possible—is much more likely to help get the siblings off to a friendly start. Talk to your older child about the baby's needs and moods—whether the baby is feeling tired or hungry, what his crying means, what he seems to enjoy. It particularly helps to show your firstborn that the baby likes looking at him. Your firstborn has, as you know, a huge appetite for attention, especially now that he's feeling a bit insecure. Try sitting down on your child's level and saying something like, "She likes looking at you." "I think he's watching you. Can you see him looking?" "He won't smile when you're yelling because it makes him a bit upset." "Listen to little Josh; he wants his bottle." Anny kept up this running conversation about the fussing baby with her three-year-old Eric:

> Eric, do you think he's hungry? Or is he just waiting for his bath? Shall we roll him over and see if he likes going on his tummy? I think we'd better hurry up and bathe him. Can you help me with the bathwater?

Eric peered at his brother and called his name, and his mother warmly responded to his efforts: "That's right! You talk to him and cheer him up." The baby eventually stopped crying, and Eric beamed with pride.

When you ask your preschooler what should be done about the baby's crying, be prepared for some striking advice. "Cut him up for firewood!" "Give her some chocolate!" "Give him to the garbage men." "Send her back to hospital and get another one!" were some of the babycare ideas offered by preschoolers in our study. Keep your sense of humor and don't worry about the more extreme suggestions. They don't necessarily imply aggression ahead. You can help diffuse some of your firstborn's hostility or jealousy with jokes about the difficulties the new baby is causing both of you. Comments such as "Oh, he likes being around you. I think you can cheer him up" are always welcome, and so is reassurance for your eldest that *he* is special, clever, funny, and *loved*.

When they are encouraged to do "real" things to care for the baby, preschoolers often blossom with pleasure and pride. Don't overlook how really helpful they can be fetching diapers, lotion, or bottles. As a mother of twins and a firstborn only eighteen months older, I learned that even my two-year-old was a real help when my hands were full. In one of the families I observed, twenty-six-month-old Penny rushed over when her mother asked her "Are you going to come and help me, Penny? I'm not doing very well, am I!" Penny beamed with pride when *she* managed to get baby Harry first to burp, then to look at her!

Preschoolers are delighted when they can catch the baby's attention. Show them what the baby likes to look at, and how to hold bright objects just a foot or so from his face so he's likely to see it. When a preschooler gets the baby to look at something, he begins to "see" the baby as a person, to understand what he likes and dislikes, and to care for him in a new way. These precious moments are the beginning of a real relationship. As the weeks go by, the baby will become a better and better audience for your firstborn, and that's a real pleasure for your oldest—and for you! There are few things more heartwarming to parents than the sight of their older child and their baby staring delightedly into each other's eyes.

Be prepared for escalating demands.

Your firstborn will probably become most demanding when you're caring for the baby. It is when you pick up the baby to feed, when you start bathing him and have your hands full, or when you are lost in that new love affair gazing at your tiny one that your first will begin to whine, wail, call for you to come to him, or do something he knows is forbidden. Acts of deliberate naughtiness are *much* more frequent when parents are occupied with the new baby, and, not surprisingly, conflict between parent and firstborn soars at these times; demands and requests also shoot up. He'll ask for a drink, for the toy that's out of his reach; he'll say he needs to be taken to the toilet, that he is stuck on his puzzle, that his tummy hurts, that he wants his shoes on to go outside. The requests and the ingenuity he displays may seem endless. What he really wants, of course, is *you*, and your attention.

It can be especially hard to remain patient and loving at these moments. But it may be some help to be prepared for them. When you sit down to feed the baby, have a drink ready for your eldest, a book or crayons to give him; if he's at the potty stage, put the potty right by you, so he can sit on it without your having to interrupt the feeding. Encourage your four- or five-year-old to play his favorite board game or puzzle next to you while you feed the baby. Many mothers encourage their eldest to come and cuddle up close while they breastfeed or give the baby a bottle, or they make the feeding a time for reading (ask your firstborn to turn the pages) or talking. You can, with a little patience and preparation, turn feedings from battlegrounds into times of special closeness.

It's fine to breastfeed.

Relatives, other mothers, or even child-care books, may warn you not to breastfeed because it is traumatic for your firstborn to see the usurper suckling at your breast. Don't listen to them. There is simply no good evidence for this. Clearly children are interested, curious, and surprised the first time they see their mothers breastfeed. Some may even be jealous the first few times, but this is uncommon. Treat the feedings as completely natural; don't seek privacy or try to hide when you nurse. It would *not* help your firstborn if you give the impression there's something secret and private you want to do with the baby from which he's excluded.

Some mothers find breastfeeding difficult when their firstborn is very eager to get close and involved. If you want to be alone with your new baby, if you feel that it is a precious and intimate time, the intrusion of your older child can be hard to take. You will need all your reserves of patience and good humor when your older child barges in, wanting to lean all over you and the baby, wanting to kiss and finger you and the baby, and to bounce and rock the bed while you try to nurse.

However your older child reacts, remember that breastfeeding *does* take a lot of time and energy—you'll be constantly at it in the first week or so, and it is crucial to get enough rest. Be prepared to do little but eat, sleep, and nurse!

Think like a preschooler.

Keeping your firstborn happy while you are caring for the baby also involves thinking up distractions for him that he'll enjoy even though you can't sit down and play. Try to put yourself in the mind of your firstborn to figure out what will amuse him. Toddlers or preschoolers are fascinated with *pretend* play, for instance, and this can be a lifesaver for a mom whose hands are full. My eighteen-month-old daughter discovered the huge excitement of make-believe just at the time her twin brothers were born, and it was a godsend. I could sit feeding both boys, *playing with her* as she fetched "cake" [wooden blocks] and we both pretended to eat, or she put her "baby" to bed (a beloved weird blue futuristic doll given her by her grandmother), and we both sang bedtime songs to the favored blue "baby."

Mothers who know what delights their children can find all sorts of unexpected distractions when their own hands are full. I really admired how Tina, mother of twenty-month-old Evan, averted a disaster looming at baby bathtime when she suggested that he might try poking a barrette he had found through the holes of a clogged soapdish. It was *exactly* the kind of thing he enjoyed—a perfect twenty-month-old activity—and with happy absorption he played at the game for a good fifteen minutes, while she successfully got the baby bathed.

The same general point—to think yourself into what your firstborn especially likes and finds interesting—applies of course even if your firstborn is four, five, or six. You know what books, games, and jokes she likes right now; the time to get these out is when you're going to be busy with the baby. Luckily it's very easy to share jokes and stories with a talkative, sophisticated four- or five-year-old, even if your hands are full.

Get help if you can.

Enlist all the help you can find for the first few weeks. You'll be lucky if you get anything like enough sleep for quite a while. Studies show that many mothers are still getting less than five hours sleep in twenty-four at three weeks after the new baby is born. Couple that with the demands and contrariness of the older children and you have a recipe for exhaustion and stress, as Alice found out: "It was just such hard work that first couple of weeks.

I didn't realize how hard it would be. I expect some of the trouble I had with Colin [her firstborn] was to do with my just being *exhausted*."

The practical message is—get as much help as possible to keep yourself going. Fay regrets that she didn't ask her husband Jim to take some time off when the second baby came. As it happened, Jim brought Fay home from the hospital at noon, stayed a couple of hours, and then went back to work at four P.M., leaving her alone with the very lively toddler and the new and wakeful baby. By Fay's own account, she was hysterical by six-thirty, and called him for help. Home he came for an hour, then went back to his office to catch up on his work. Fay's first day at home with two kids was memorably awful. But it would have gone a lot more smoothly had Jim been available all day, instead of just on an emergency basis.

If your husband can't take time off, as is often the case, friends can help in all sorts of ways, both for moral support and more practically by doing shopping for you, baby-sitting, coming to have coffee with you. One mom had help twice a week from a neighbor who simply took over cooking the evening meal. "Thank God for the phone and my friends," as another mother put it succinctly. If you are lucky enough to have relatives nearby, now is the moment to pull family ties.

Hired help, even if only for very brief but regular periods, can provide welcome relief. One mother spent her savings on *one hour of help from five P.M. to six P.M.*, three days a week. She was lucky to find a woman who worked all day in an office and loved coming to play with and bathe a toddler and baby after work. For the mom, it felt like heaven to cook dinner in (comparative) peace.

DIVIDING YOUR TIME BETWEEN TWO

You and your spouse may want to spend some time working out the balance of who looks after which child. In some families a specially close father-firstborn relationship means it makes sense for him to take care of her most of the time, while you deal with the new baby. But if your firstborn wants *you* most right now, conflict may arise: You may want to spend time alone with your new baby and worry you are missing out on some special "bonding period." You feel torn between the two who need you, and want to nurture both. There is, however, absolutely no need to fear that you and your new baby will not become warmly and securely attached just because you are spending less time alone with her than you did with your first baby as a newborn. Your new baby will feel comfort and learn your face, your ways, your voice, even if you're holding your eldest with the other arm at the same time. And you will certainly find plenty of moments to be alone with the baby.

If your eldest is at preschool or daycare, then there's usually less of a problem about dividing your time between your two children. Your older child's nap, if he still takes one, can become your "baby" time, when you focus on your new baby—unless, of course, the new one is also asleep. If that's the case, at least you, too, can get some rest. But however you arrange things, don't be anxious that your new baby will fail to relate to you because you are occupied with your firstborn. It won't happen.

Finally—if you can, relax and *don't* worry about everyone! As one mother commented when her children were four and six years old: "When I look back on those first weeks, I see that I should have relaxed more. It helped when I finally realized that I'd been *worrying* too much about all of them! In the long run, we've all done pretty well together!"

The first few weeks can be a tough time for you, but things change fast, and most exciting of all you'll see a real relationship beginning to grow between the children. We will turn next to those changes in the following months.

SUMMARY OF SURVIVAL TIPS

• *Give your first lots of attention.*
This is essential, even if she's being whiny and difficult.
• *Keep to a routine.*
Make sure the daily pattern of meals, naps, and outings stays pretty similar, especially if you have a two- to three-year-old.
• *Make those visitors pay attention to your oldest.*
Remind them (ahead of time if possible) about your needy firstborn.
• *Limit visitors.*
If your firstborn gets wildly excited or difficult when the visitors come, tell them to wait a couple of weeks.
• *Let your oldest help with the baby.*
Make him feel part of the family by "helping"—as long as he's interested.
• *Be prepared for demands.*
Your firstborn will make more and more demands, especially when you're trying to care for the baby. Get distractions ready beforehand. Try to imagine what he would especially like.

- *Find help if at all possible.*
  Now is the time to call on husbands, grandparents, neighbors, friends to help. Don't hesitate to ask them.

Chapter 6

LIVING TOGETHER: THE FIRST YEAR

You have been home for a couple of weeks, and the drama of the birth has receded. (So, too, probably, have the offers of help.) Now you are left confronting the very different demands and needs of your baby and your firstborn, as well as the pleasures and problems of coping with a family of four. In general, although life certainly gets much easier as the weeks and months go by, your elder child will *still* need special love and attention. As the baby gets more assertive and more charming, the green-eyed monster of jealousy often looms larger and larger.

This chapter focuses on the most common problems that arise in the year or so following your second born's birth, as well as how you can best handle these difficulties.

COPING WITH TWO: THE FIRST SIX MONTHS

Making the Balancing Act Work

The requirements of a young baby—feeding more or less on demand, immediate attention at unpredictable moments, possibly quite a lot of carrying and cuddling in the evening—all add up to a changeable, uncertain schedule. But a two- to four-year-old child wants a familiar and dependable routine. A baby introduces endless interruptions and frustrations into the older one's time with you. Your firstborn has just gotten your attention and has you sitting on the floor to play a game, when the baby wakes and cries, and off you go again. This is very hard on a child. Sudden changes and a seemingly undependable mother and father are major causes of stress for firstborn children.

Making the balancing act work can be a challenge. What are the most important requirements to keep things on an even keel?

Here are five good candidates:

- Enough sleep for everyone, and a reasonable bedtime routine. The tired toddler or preschooler who is *not* difficult is a rarity.
- As much time with your older one as can be managed—or as he seems to want.
- A *stable* daily routine that helps everyone, including baby-sitters, grandparents, and so on.
- Time for you to recover your spirits—which probably means time away from under-fives.

- Contact with other mothers and fathers who know what life is like with two little ones.

Let's look at each of these candidates, and see how you can improve your chances of achieving them.

SLEEPTIME SCHEDULES

Getting Your Firstborn Off to Sleep

> The worst thing is that Troy won't go to sleep—bedtimes are a nightmare now—I'm exhausted because the baby's still waking a lot at night, and it feels like the last straw that we go through is this obstacle course every night to get him to bed. We have trouble at naptime too.
>
> CAREY, MOTHER OF THREE-YEAR-OLD TROY

Whatever your firstborn's age, it is a good idea to try to stick to a calm, regular routine at bedtime. The classic progression from supper to bathtime to book and bed works well for lots of kids. Don't let him get too overtired or too overstimulated before bedtime if you can possibly avoid it. Tired children have trouble making the shift to sleep. Even if your firstborn is cheerful all day and apparently doesn't need much sleep, stick to a quiet, early bedtime—*you* need it even if he doesn't. If he is only a toddler, include a regular naptime too. Even if he doesn't sleep at naptime, a quiet twenty minutes looking at books—like children get at daycare—may make the afternoons smoother. If naptimes are a problem, try lying down with him (unless he's such a dynamo that he makes it impossible for you to get any rest). Tell him you'll have one book together, then both close your eyes to sleep; or try letting him take his nap in a different place from his crib: on a sofa, with a "special" coverlet, for instance. It sometimes also helps to establish a special naptime routine: A cassette with a story can be left on while he lies in his crib, or a piece of music that you listen to together.

If your child is between two and three and fights naptime, see how she does during the day without one. If she's happy, playing cheerfully, not whining *too* much, and doesn't fall apart when frustrated about something, she probably doesn't need the extra sleep. But you may want to stick to a "quiet time" after lunch in any case, when she lies down and looks at books. And, if she stops napping, you can probably get her to bed earlier at night.

Waking in the Night

If your first child started sleeping badly when the new baby came home, this problem will almost certainly end by the time the baby is six to eight months old. Not always, of course: Some first-borns keep up their lively nightlife of ups and downs for well over a year. Regular waking at night often means that parents fall into a pattern of going in to soothe their firstborn, which sometimes results in hours of playing in the small hours. If this has happened to you, it is well worth trying the strategies recommended in some of the books on children's sleep problems. One of the most successful is the "let him cry for five minutes" technique.

The basic idea here is to limit the kind of contact you give your child each night, and to get him to settle himself back to sleep. The first step is to go in to check on him when he cries in the night, talk soothingly to reassure him, stroke him, and tuck him up again in bed—comfort him, but don't pick him up.

Then—and this is the hard part—you leave the room, even if he's not yet asleep, and you stay out, even if he's crying. In *Solve Your Child's Sleep Problems*, Richard Ferber suggests that you try to stay out for around fifteen minutes, then, if necessary, go in and repeat the "checking"—but again, don't pick him up. If you cannot stand to hear him cry for more than five minutes, then go in after five, but the key is this: The next night when he wakes and cries, let him cry for a little longer before you go in. Each night, increase the time before you go in to check. Once children learn that they won't be picked up and played with, which usually happens after just a few nights, then they do begin to settle themselves and fall back asleep if they wake.

The more consistent and firm you can be (and it is very tough on you too!), the quicker he'll learn to fall back to sleep on his own. This commonly recommended technique works pretty well for most children. And when he does stop waking, you will feel transformed!

TIME WITH YOUR FIRSTBORN

It's a simple fact that life is never again the same for the displaced firstborn and that parental attention to most first children *never regains the level it had been at before the new baby's birth*. It's not surprising that many firstborns get moody and difficult as the months go by (more on that below). But there are ways to minimize the upset and preserve at least some special time for you and your firstborn to share. It can help if you try to limit the interruptions to your time together. Here's what one mother did:

> I kept the baby in the kitchen with me and my first one:
> Having a crib there and a baby seat meant that at least I

didn't have to keep running off to the bedroom, or dragging my poor older one upstairs with me every time the baby cried.

It's a good solution. Another solution is to carry the baby in a sling or snuggly on your back or front while you focus on your firstborn. Be wary, however, that some children, even sophisticated four-year-olds, may be jealous of the baby's "privileged" position in the sling.

Try to find other ways of spending time with your first *on his own*. If you can get a baby-sitter, take him out for a quick meal (Dad may enjoy coming along too!). Or leave the baby with a neighbor or grandmother while you take him off somewhere he especially likes. Fetch him from preschool or school on his own if you can. Go to the library to choose books for him without the baby always in tow.

GETTING THE NEW BABY ON A SCHEDULE

I fed my first baby pretty much on demand, but then came the twins and I found that I just had to push them toward more of a regular feeding schedule than I had with my first child. Many parents find that their second baby can hang on a bit more for feedings as the weeks go by. If she wakes an hour or so after a feeding, she's probably not hungry, and you can try to get her to wait for a feeding a bit later by distracting her, or by getting your first to "talk" to her and make faces. Of course, some babies are much easier than others to get into a regular feeding and sleeping routine. If your second is an obliging and easygoing baby, you'll find you can even out the feeding intervals within the first six weeks or so with a bit of patience. If you have a very irregular feeder, you may have to pass up that plan for another couple of months.

Structure to the day gives everyone, and especially your children, a sense of security and predictability. It's a help for baby-sitters, and anyone helping you too. Napping and sleeping schedules are a key element in organizing your day. So by all means try to find a schedule that works for all of you—and stick to it.

TAKING TIME FOR YOURSELF

Getting a brief break from your children, lovely as they are, to do something that's definitely *your* entertainment is very important. For working mothers, this is especially hard. You often feel every minute that's not taken up by work should be spent with the children. Yet taking some time for yourself can be a lifesaver that keeps you happy and better able to enjoy them fully when you are with them.

Of course every parent finds *real release* in his or her own way. Here are some ideas:

- Leave the children with a friend once a week while you take an aerobics class.
- Regularly once every two weeks, get your hair done or treat yourself to a manicure or a facial.
- Physical exercise: whatever you can find and enjoy.
- Go shopping *alone*.

SUPPORT FROM OTHER PARENTS WHO HAVE BEEN THROUGH IT AND SURVIVED

Talking about the trials and tantrums with friends who also have young children is a real help; it can give you back your sense of humor about the absurdities of life with two kids under six, and it can show you there's light at the end of the tunnel. It may also be worthwhile to join a mother-toddler group, even if your toddler ends up refusing to get off your knee or fights with the other kids over toys. One mother, new to a small town, started her own mother-and-toddler group in the local church hall. "It saved my life," she comments frankly.

GETTING ORGANIZED

Does there come a point in your day when again and again you feel the chaos is overwhelming? For some mothers it's repeated trips to the grocery store with two kids who have to be dressed and then monitored in the store. For others it is the awful early morning rush to get kids to school and daycare and get themselves to work.

Once you've identified the bad times in your day, think about how to get the chaos under control. For instance, if it is the shopping with them that's awful, develop a routine that avoids it as much as possible:

- Plan to include quick visits to the store on the way to or from work, or after dropping your firstborn at school or daycare.
- Get your husband to call you every day just before he leaves work to see if there's anything he can pick up for you.

If you have never been a terribly well-organized person, now is the time to begin (necessity is the mother of invention). Make lists obsessively. Do as much as you can on weekends, when your spouse can look after the kids.

You can help relieve the morning frenzy by doing some advance planning. Think about it the night before, and pare down to the bare essentials what will need to be done in the morning. Get as much ready as you can the night before. Lists, again, may help. Some parents even organize themselves on a week-by-week basis, sitting down on Sunday night to plan for the next week's set of doctor's visits, meals, school outings. That may sound a bit obsessive to you, but it is a great way to organize others to help you—you can give them lots of advance notice that you need help next Wednesday, and so on.

GETTING OUT OF THE HOUSE

Especially for mothers who don't work outside the home, simply getting out with the two children rather than being stuck at home all day can help you keep happy and sane. Here's how Ashley, mother of three-year-old Kay and six-month-old Randy, found that "a quick walk—even on gray days—took my mind off their demands, and my preschooler loved it. A sling and a stroller kept us all going. And it was a great way of getting my baby to sleep."

It's not always that easy—even if you live somewhere with good places to walk that are easily accessible. You need a strong back if you go the sling-and-stroller route; if you use a double stroller, be prepared for how unmaneuverable the thing is (especially when fully loaded with children), and for unhelpful passersby who glare at you.

Strategies for Longer Outings

Going on trips—even relatively brief ones, is a strikingly different business now that you have two. One mother said that packing up for a weekend at the ocean was like getting ready for a space mission—and she pointed out that after all the work there's always the possibility that the children will be miserable once you get there. However exhausting it may be, careful advance preparation is essential to an even moderately successful trip. Remember to pack diapers, juice, wipes, a change of clothes, and so forth, *and* the special toy or "comfort object" for your firstborn. For long car trips, bring along cassettes with your firstborn's favorite songs and stories; if possible, tie his toys onto the car seat so they don't fall out of reach. One father makes special "trip packs" for his two children—he includes things for them to do once the trip is under way. Be sure you have snacks for those children who fall to pieces without sustenance by their regular mealtimes. And try your best to maintain some semblance of their regular schedule. If you have a child who can't keep going without a nap midday, don't risk missing it. In a pinch he can sleep in his stroller or in the car. The same is true, of course, for the baby.

CHANGES IN YOUR FIRSTBORN

After the first couple of weeks at home, you'll probably notice some changes in your firstborn's behavior—some of these welcome, others not so welcome.

New Signs of Jealousy

Lots of firstborn children show renewed signs of jealousy when their baby siblings reach three or four months old, and blossom into charming, responsive people in their own right. Parents and grandparents fall in love—all too obviously—with these delightful, smiling, cooing babies. The firstborn child who has previously tolerated and even enjoyed the baby suddenly has a real competitor to contend with. You are quite likely to hear remarks like "I don't *like* her" at this stage. The baby may also get pinching, poking, and cuddles that become much too tight for his comfort. Preschoolers and even five- and six-year-olds are sometimes quite frank about the pleasure it gives them to provoke the baby to tears. Calley, mother of three-year-old Sharon, heard a strangled cry from her baby's bedroom and rushed in to find Sharon stuffing a blanket into the baby's mouth. Grabbing the baby, she angrily asked her scared but defiant daughter, "Why did you do that?" "Because it's fun to hurt him!" was her daughter's reply. If your firstborn is old enough to talk about what he's feeling, it can be a great help. Vera found discussions with six-year-old Ben to be enormously helpful when he became particularly difficult with his four-month-old sister: "Once I did figure out that Ben was acting out his jealous feelings, I could talk to him about it. After one particularly bad episode, a light finally went on in my brain and I said to him, 'Do you feel sad because Mom and Dad are paying lots of attention to Sarah?' He nodded his head yes, and when I asked why, he said, 'Because nobody loves me anymore.' This, of course, broke my heart and I was able to reassure him that we loved him more than ever. I think the very fact that he could articulate his feelings so well made all the difference. It is clear to me that the firstborn's need for love and reassurance never ends."

Fears, Worries, and Ritualized Behaviors

As the months go by, your firstborn's need for attention and reassurance of your continued love can show up in ways that may strike you as odd and even rather perverse. Since things seem to have settled down somewhat, you may not initially connect these behaviors with the baby's presence, but that is often what underlies them. For instance, your firstborn's general level of crankiness and worrying is quite likely to increase. Irrational fears too, for example, that objects will get broken or lost or that a pet will die, often become more common during the first year, especially among children under five. Cherry noticed a marked upswing in the anxiety level of her three-year-old, Wayne: "He's very concerned about losing things, and about me hurting myself. Or about dangers. He 'reports' to his dad about me, or to me about his dad, if we've done dangerous things—'naughty things,' he calls it." About a third of firstborn children show an increase in very specific fears or worries over the course of the first year. Three- and four-year-olds who don't have new siblings also frequently develop new fears—so some of this is age-related. But, interestingly, age does not seem to be a factor in engendering fears for firstborns with new babies in the house. This behavior is a sign that the older siblings feel increasingly insecure over the realization that the new addition is there "for keeps." So if you notice such fears, you need not feel that your child is developing some bizarrely exceptional behavior. One three-year-old would not go into the street if he saw a cat; another was terrified of water in the bath, another of the dark, still another ran screaming from the noise of the vacuum cleaner. Deal with each fear calmly; comfort her, respect her wishes, and try to avoid the situation that frightens her if you can. You can help her come to terms with what frightens her by very gradually exposing her to the source of the fear.

For example, if your two-year-old suddenly is frightened of going into the bath, give up baths for a bit; make do with sponge baths (for a while), then gradually reintroduce bathtime. Start with one inch of water in the tub; when she's comfortable with stepping into that, increase the level to another inch, and so on. If the water rushing down the drain at the end of the bath terrifies her, take her out of the bathroom before the water is drained and don't drain the bath till she's out of earshot. When she feels calmer about going in the bath, you can show her a little water draining out of the sink, and take it from there by gradually increasing the amount that she sees swooshing down the drain.

An increase in dependent behavior often surfaces at this stage too: The older child will begin to insist on being dressed by one parent or the other, or on being taken to the toilet, or on being fed. And she may up her demands for the *ritual* at bedtime and mealtime. Your firstborn might insist at meals that you put her food in a special dish, that each member of the family must use a particular place mat, and that you blow on her food three times before she'll eat it. At bedtime she might refuse to sleep unless you or her father kiss all her teddies, then kiss her between each bar of the crib, and leave the door open at a specific angle, with the light on outside. If you don't want the rituals to get extended and more elaborate, set clear limits to the sequence and stick to them.

By no means do all children show these signs of worry and upset. Emotionally intense children who tend to be moody or anxious anyway are most likely to show the increased worrying or fearful or ritualized behavior. Also, children who react to their sibling's arrival by *withdrawing* into themselves, sitting for long periods sucking their thumbs or clutching their comfort objects, are especially likely to increase in moodiness, and to seem anxious or worried.

If you have one of these children, it's worth making an extra effort to show him you still love him, to play with him as often as you can, and to lavish extra love and attention, not just immediately after the new baby comes, but over the next year or so.

Toilet-Training Breakdowns and Other Trials

The problems that cropped up when you first came home with the new baby—toilet training breakdown and excessive demands, disheartening tests of parental patience and humor—do, I promise you, decrease for the very great majority of families around six months after the baby is born. If you are facing these problems, patience and reassurance rather than punishment are what are called for. Ease up for a month or so on what you expect in the way of dryness by day and by night. And give him lots of praise when he begins to regain control. These breakdowns in toilet training are an expression of general insecurity, so the more you can keep a calm, stable routine, and pay lots of attention to your firstborn, the quicker you're likely to get back to a happier life together. Time alone often takes care of the problems without any further intervention from you.

"We tried everything," said one mother about her attempts to deal with her older daughter's contrariness, misdeeds, and aggression after the baby came. "We gave her extra attention, scolded her, took away her treats, but none of it helped. Nothing seemed to work. Finally, she just kind of grew out of it."

HITTING AND HURTING

Trouble with Toddlers

"Nicole was very unhappy about the baby from day one!" says Anna of her angry two-year-old daughter. "From the fourth week after Brian arrived home from the hospital, Nicole was in trouble for hurting him. She would hug him really hard, till he cried, she would sit on his head, and she would poke him. When he was a month old, she would pinch him, pile toys on him when he was in his crib. When he cried she hit him." Anna was in despair. She'd guessed before Brian was born that there might be some difficulties with Nicole, but her attempts to *hurt* Brian were so upsetting.

If your toddler is behaving like Nicole, what can you do to protect your baby and to help your firstborn stop being aggressive?

First, never leave them together alone, out of your sight—not even for a minute. Make sure the room your baby sleeps in is firstborn-proof, with a gate.

Second, if you can, see what sets the hurting or teasing off. In Nicole's case, she was most likely to be aggressive when she was alone with her mom and baby Brian, with no other people around to distract her, or when her mom was very much occupied with Brian. Nicole was a very bright, easily bored child, and Anna felt that a combination of jealousy, restlessness, and boredom precipitated the violence. What helped in the short term was to find things to occupy Nicole during feeding or bathtimes. "We did a lot of prevention," Anna notes. "We tried to arrange things so she didn't just have to sit there while I was doing things with him." When Dad was around, he tried to get involved *before* the trouble began: When Nicole had her father to herself she was much happier.

If aggression breaks out despite your preventive measures, here are some ways to cope:

Have a firm rule that there is to be no hitting.

You must have some immediate response to the hitting that makes clear you won't allow it. Put the toddler who hit the baby in a different room. Tell him firmly that there's to be *no* hitting, and *no* hurting. Explain that he has hurt the baby, that no one hits in this family. Show him you are serious about it, but stay calm. The violence will decrease only if you have a regular, consistent, very firm response. Have a firm rule too that if toys are used as weapons, they get taken away.

With toddlers and preschoolers, the aggression is likely to be mostly about *getting your attention*. So if your response is to say "Oh I understand that you're upset, so I'll play with you now," you're actually *supporting* the aggression and virtually assuring that it will happen again. Of course you'll respond to that need for attention with extra love and reassurance, but do it later. Don't sit down and play with her immediately after she has hit the baby.

Keep your own anger and distress out of the picture

You may feel like a shewolf defending her cub, outraged and furious; you may also feel guilty—that your firstborn is so upset by the displacement that he's jealous enough to hit and hurt. You'll probably be surprised by the strength of both those feelings. But showing those feelings by being angry or very upset, or overcompensating by rushing to smother your firstborn with attention, won't help to calm the toddler *or* the baby. So try not to yell at your firstborn. Stay calm, firm, and serious about the message of no hitting.

Trouble with preschoolers and other firstborns

The same principles used with aggressive toddlers apply to older firstborn children: Keep the firstborn and the baby apart, try to see what precipitates the trouble, and *have a firm rule of no violence.* One advantage you have with articulate older children is that you can communicate more easily with them. You can express the rule more complexly: "Anytime you are upset and angry, come and tell me about it. It's fine to say how you feel. But in this family there won't be any hitting and hurting."

When your preschooler does hit the baby, put the aggressor in a different room, or give him a time-out. If the hitting continues, then follow up by taking away a privilege (that TV show, that planned trip to the mall). Remember not to make loss-of-privilege threats that you don't carry out. Children learn very fast indeed that you won't act on your threats and these cease to be a deterrent. And don't hesitate to act fast if there is hitting, kicking, or poking. As one mother who has calmly brought up four children close in age states bluntly: "If the baby is being hurt or frightened or hit, I wouldn't wait to stop what is happening any more than I would wait if a toddler was wandering out into the busy street."

Talking About It

Talking it out with your troubled preschooler may help. Try asking leading questions or even naming his feelings for him. "I think maybe you don't like it when I'm feeding Johnny. *Whenever* you feel that way come and tell me—and we'll do something together . . . come on and give me the hugest hug you can!"

It can provide a welcome release for your older child—and for you—to talk about what he dislikes about the baby. Ron, father of three-year-old Jilly, admits that: "It's hard when she goes on and on about wishing the baby wasn't there, but we've got so we can laugh about it together now, and somehow that makes it easier." Try to turn her distress into a shared joke—tell her, for instance, you know just what she's going to say—it will also make your firstborn feel understood and valued.

While your immediate response to hitting will help to decrease it, you must really address what is underlying that violence if you want it to stop. If your firstborn preschooler is acting out because he's unsure of your love and attention, confronting him angrily is not going to help. You are, after all, bigger, cleverer, and less vulnerable than he—even if he's a relatively sophisticated four- or five-year-old. *You* can find a way around this problem more easily than he can. Think about how he is feeling, and use what you know about his special needs and wishes to find some way of reassuring and cheering him.

A NEW KIND OF LOVING

Lots of parents find that their older children become even more loving, especially with their dads, over these months. Surprisingly, age is not really a significant factor in this new surge of affection. As with the signs of upset, a child's personality seems to be the determining factor in this response. It is more common in those children who are very intense in their emotions—full of laughter and tears, lurching from excitement to misery. If you have one of these children, enjoy that affection and cuddling even when it comes at inconvenient times—don't turn her away.

FATHERS AND FIRSTBORNS

"Daddy do it!" "Here's my daddy!" The firstborn often feels an increased attachment to Dad over the course of the year following the new sibling's arrival. You'll see more love and affection and huge excitement when he comes home. And often the feeling is mutual. Many fathers find it is easier to get involved with their first children as they get older. Barry says: "I do feel more and more close with Tommy. I don't know how much it's to do with him growing up, or the baby taking his mom's time—but I do find I'm doing more things with him—and it's great."

This "special relationship" may mean that your elder becomes particularly annoyed when her father plays with that usurper, the baby. Children often watch like eagles when their fathers play with the second one. Some of the upset you saw in the first two weeks also resurfaces. And (this can be so irritating to mothers!) they're often far more compliant with their father than with their mother. As Barry's wife Cora says, "His father only has to *speak*. I threaten, and he ignores me." Firstborn children commonly become more upset if their father is angry with them than if their mother scolds them.

For many first children, a strong and increasingly warm relationship with Dad can provide a huge emotional support as they grapple with the uncertainty of life with a sibling. You can make the most of this by seeing that your child and her father have time together *without* the baby getting all the attention. Bedtime stories that are a special father-and-daughter feature of the day, bathtime that is solely Dad's responsibility, trips to the park without the baby, will all help.

GOING BACK TO WORK

The return to work after a second child can be extremely stressful for parents, and for their firstborn. As Arlie Hochschild reports in *The Second Shift*, for some working parents the firstborn strains the couple's energy, but the secondborn provokes a crisis. She emphasizes three facets of the crisis that stand out in the first year or so—the *mother exhaustion* factor, the *firstborn reaction*, and the *load-sharing stress*.

Once a mom goes back to work, the burdens of dealing with *two* young children and keeping the household running (both of which usually fall largely on her shoulders) on top of the demands of her work can be intolerable, especially if her sleep is interrupted. Vera was surprised at how much harder the return to work was after the new baby arrived than it had been the first time with only one child: "The return to work with two kids was a more difficult adjustment than I'd imagined. I'd gotten used to a certain level of physical independence in Ben, but six-year-olds are extremely demanding of attention nevertheless. Now with the baby, I find that I'm always tending to one of them, so basically I don't stop going from six in the morning till about nine at night, when they are both finally asleep—at which point I collapse. I hadn't counted on this much exhaustion—and I'm one of the lucky ones, with a very helpful husband and a baby-sitter who manages the cleaning and laundry!"

Vera adds that when she found herself attempting to shampoo her hair in the shower with her husband's shaving cream, she realized how "spaced out" with exhaustion she had become. Lots of working mothers have similar tales, told with grim humor, of the months after their second child joins the family.

Mothers at the battlefront recommend these ways of coping

with the strains of being a working mother with two little ones:

- Cutting back on work hours: Part-time work, if you can manage it, may be the ideal solution. However, the money from your full-time job may well be needed, and part-time work to some mothers may feel like defeat and lower their sense of self-esteem. Arlie Hochschild cites a mother who after reducing hours at work felt depressed, "fat," "just a housewife"; in the supermarket she wanted to call down the aisles, "I'm an MBA! I'm an MBA!" Some mothers find work is an exhilarating release from the tensions of home, and cutting back on their work time ends up making them unhappy. The children pick up on this, so no one really gains anything.
- Cutting back on housework: Most mothers end up doing this anyway whether they have a job or not. Some find it adds to a sense of being out of control; others welcome the sense of *not caring* about housework.
- Cutting back on child care. It's fine not to bathe the kids every night, for instance.

  However, taking shortcuts on the *emotional* care of children is clearly not a good idea, especially when they are at a particularly vulnerable stage.
- Getting more help. This is, of course, a good idea, if it is at all feasible. See if you can arrange for a sitter to do some housework. And, of course, your husband must pitch in.

  Load-sharing between mother and father is clearly a very big issue, which couples solve (or try to solve) in a variety of ways according to the balance that suits them and their relationship. I'll simply underline the importance, and the rarity, of equity here.

Next, the *firstborn factor.* It is quite common for parents to notice an upsurge of difficult behavior or jealousy from their firstborn just after they return to work. Vera certainly picked this up in Ben's reactions to her return to work:

> Though Ben claimed, in his tough six-year-old way, that he didn't care that I was going back to work, I think he really did. And he certainly wasn't used to having to share my attention when I got home. I continued a six P.M. nursing for about a month after I started back. Inevitably Ben would bring me a book to read just as I'd settled in with the baby. Luckily reading to him and nursing the baby was something I could manage.

These strategies might help you cope with your child's problematic behaviors in the months after your return to work:

- Try to be there for key moments of your firstborn's day, like the morning-breakfast-dressing stage, and the evening games, supper, bath, and bedtime routine. Lots of working mothers keep their firstborn up late in the evening, encouraging a long nap in the day, so they'll have more time to spend with him. For toddlers this can mean that you are around for a sizable proportion of their waking hours.
- Try to keep up with what's happened in his day that matters to *him.* Call home if you can. One of the real problems for working parents—especially for those with toddlers and two-year-olds—is that they can lose touch if they don't share much of their child's day. This can make it harder to enjoy him, and to manage him, when you *are* together. Obviously, if your firstborn is older, you can talk to her and ask her directly about her

day. With a younger child, you can be sure to ask the sitter, and talk to the daycare people about what your child is doing, any new games she is playing, or new friends she is making.

• Try to focus on *him* in the mornings instead of letting your work worries preoccupy you at home, and *enjoy* your time with him in the evenings. Related to this—try to plan some private escape routes for yourself when you are organizing the return to work. It is in everybody's interest for you to be happy.

For parents who have baby-sitters who come to their homes, it is particularly important to choose one who will be sympathetic to your firstborn's reactions, and who in later months will handle fights and conflict between your two children in a way that meshes with your own. Some sitters prefer babies to older children and let it show in their behavior toward your child. Bear this in mind when interviewing potential baby-sitters. If you already have a baby-sitter, it is worth discussing all these issues with her, so she knows your own views and feelings about how to handle any difficult behavior from your firstborn, and how to manage the increasingly complex interactions between your two children.

WHEN THE BABY BECOMES A TODDLER

When baby siblings become active, mobile, and assertive, the family dynamics often change, again quite markedly. The baby who could be conveniently parked out of the way of your firstborn's precious toys, elaborate constructions with blocks, and his pretend games is now a major demolition agent. On the flip side, she is becoming more and more charming, with a whole new set of skills for getting adult attention—and adoration. The potential for trouble between siblings skyrockets as a result. You will be increasingly called upon to manage conflict between them instead of simply dealing with firstborn distress. For many, this is where the challenge of parenthood really begins.

Here are some ways to rise to these challenges with a toddler and a preschooler. (Chapters Seven and Eight cover conflict and rivalry between children who are both into the preschool period and beyond.)

Remove the invader.

When the baby becomes mobile and begins to spoil your firstborn's games and destroy her toys, make sure your firstborn knows that if she calls you, *you will remove the invader.* You'll avoid some direct action on her part that may have dire consequences if she is confident that you will remove the demolition agent when she asks. And make sure that you *do.*

Apply the no-hitting rule to everybody.

As the baby gets more agile and active, be sure to apply the no-hitting rule and no-using-toys-as-weapons rule *to the baby too.* Even if that swipe or poke from the baby was accidental, remove the toy from the baby and tell the baby not to hit. It is very important for your firstborn to see that the rules are applied to the invader as well as to her. And—it goes without saying—make sure you don't hit either. You are the most powerful model around.

Show you understand your firstborn's irritation.

When the baby ruins your firstborn's construction, or his carefully set-out game, let him know that you understand what a pest the baby is to him. It can help to say "Your sister *can* be such a nuisance!" or "I can see how she pesters you—even though she didn't mean to knock it down! Let's find her something else to play with." If your older takes toys from your younger—the "mine" syndrome—encourage your firstborn to find something else for the baby as a substitute.

Don't always sympathize with the baby.

Avoid showing too much sympathy for the smaller, more "helpless" (less intentionally diabolical) younger sibling. It is all too easy to do.

Try to ensure your firstborn has his own space.

It's well worth trying to make sure that your firstborn has a space where he can play quietly, uninterrupted by the toddler. And that also applies to the times when he has a friend over to play. One mom made a "secret place" for her firstborn, with a "tent" created from a tablecloth in a corner of the living room; another made a "den" under the kitchen table.

MANAGING THE DAY

Finding a good way to organize your days and schedule in some escapes remains key as the baby grows up, though the particular issues that loom large change, of course. Now, for instance, you'll be deciding how to deal with bathtimes, mealtimes, and outings for two lively kids, how to cope with new safety issues as the baby discovers the exciting debris of scissors and sharp toys left by your firstborn, and how to get two jumping jacks into bed. Dealing with most of these issues is a matter of common sense, patience, and good humor as well as individual preference, but here are some hints that have worked well in other families.

Bathtimes

Your one-year-old and her close-in-age older sibling may find bathing together to be wild fun, but for you it can be a crazily difficult time as you try to manage a slippery baby in danger of going under, a howling firstborn who wants to have all the toys and the space, and then two rapidly cooling, dripping children who both need help in being dried and clothed. One solution is to give them separate baths on alternate days.

Another is to bathe them together, putting your second born in a bathtub "anchor" that holds to the bottom with suction cups. That way they can enjoy the splashing fun without so much danger. Often, joint bathtimes turn out to be the setting for some of their friendliest games as they pour and splash water together. You can get your firstborn to show the baby how to wash herself and to splash and pour. *Don't* go out of the room, leaving them alone in the bath together, however, not even for a minute.

As for the drying problems: Have the towels and the clothes you want to put on them all ready; get your baby out first, and when she's dry and dressed, take out your older child.

Mealtimes

If you have two close in age, mealtimes can also present problems once the baby starts eating solids, especially if your firstborn still needs or wants lots of attention from you at meals. You may find it a help to get hold of a second high chair, and resort to the strategies that mothers of twins use, with two dishes of food, and two spoons at the ready. It is a great help when they both like picking up finger foods. Encourage them (subtly) to eat the same foods so you don't end up preparing two separate meals each time. If your older one eats with you and your husband, put the baby in a booster seat or high chair at the table—they like to be part of things.

Safety

Having two roaming children means you have to be sure to do a good job of childproofing the house. You simply won't be able to watch them both. And they'll each be doing different kinds of investigation of the delights of the sewing box, the medicine cabinet, the bottle of bleach. On top of that, your second one will investigate all the toys and paraphernalia left by your firstborn—and much of that is dangerous stuff. Construction kits with tiny pieces will be inserted in the mouth, sharp-edged toys will be tripped over; so don't leave them within the baby's reach. In addition, a baby can learn potentially dangerous new skills very fast indeed from watching his older sibling: how to open cupboards, unscrew bottles, cut with scissors. Enlist your firstborn's help in keeping his toys out of reach. Even if he does not pick up everything he can be reminded to be careful about the dangerous toys.

So monitor your home with great care, and make sure to place your firstborn's potentially dangerous toys up high, where his sibling can't reach them. All too soon, that sibling will be pushing chairs and climbing on them, and then almost *nothing* is safe.

Getting Out and About

When your first is still too young to walk far, two-seater strollers are certainly helpful. However, you should know that they are not always very stable. Those that load the children front and back are more likely to tip over than the side-by-side sort, especially when one child is taken out. But the side-by-side sort are very hard to maneuver, and often you can't get them through doors. All double strollers are very hard to get up and down steps, especially when loaded with kids. Be very wary of the "hitchhiker" attachments to ordinary strollers, as these can be very unstable when you have one heavy child aboard. It's best not to let your older one push the younger in the stroller—it's so easy to tip it over, baby and all.

You may choose to stick to your old stroller and put the baby in a carrier, using a frame carrier after the baby is about five months. Just remember that you're going to need a strong back as she reaches toddlerhood!

If caring for two begins to seem unbearably trying, do take your own needs seriously. Contact with other struggling parents can restore your sense of humor about the impossible demands, and help you keep things in perspective. You aren't the only one at your wit's end! And remember this is probably the hardest phase of all. One father pinned a notice above his children's beds to remind himself that "This too shall pass!" Ahead are the real pleasures of watching your children's relationship growing and changing, as we see in the next chapter.

SUMMARY OF TIPS FOR SURVIVAL

- *Talk to friends who have been through it and survived.*
  Stay in touch with others who know what it's like; this will help you keep up your hopes and your sense of humor.
- *Get help.*
  If you can afford it, brief but regular help can be a godsend. Even if it is only for an hour or so a week, it can put those demands and those diapers in a different perspective.
- *Get a break yourself.*
  If you're not working away from home, then getting a quick break from the children—especially on a regular basis—can be a great boon.

- *Get out of the house.*
  With or without them, getting out will help.
- *Keeping stable routines.*
  It's helpful to everyone if the day has a predictable pattern.
- *Continue to give your firstborn lots of attention.*
  Even when he is least appealing—that's often when he needs you most!
- *Keep your sense of humor!*

Chapter 7

THE SIBLINGS: A GROWING RELATIONSHIP

You'll see lots of changes in the interaction between your oldest and your baby over the first three to four months. Many firstborns become more involved with their siblings—friendlier, more interested—as the babies become more responsive to *them*. The two of them will find their own way of relating. Your firstborn will discover what a great audience his younger sibling can be: Here is someone always delighted by his company and easily amused by any clowning he puts on. As babies reach three to four months, they are easier for everyone to soothe and comfort, including your firstborn and this, too, helps their relationship along. On the other hand, conflict also mounts as the siblings' relationship becomes more intense and more complicated. Firstborns often have mixed feelings about their fast-growing baby siblings, and they display these mixed feelings in lots of different ways—cuddles that turn into squeezes hard enough to make the baby cry, tickling that ends up as pinching, and verbal insults are all quite common.

SMILING, SONG-AND-DANCE, AND CLOWNING

It's a great moment for many older siblings as well as for parents when babies begin to smile. For three-, four-, and five-year-olds, being able to coax a smile out of a six-week-old sibling is a source of great pride and pleasure, and gives them a new delight in the baby. So it's great if you can help your older child to elicit those smiles. Show him how the baby grins when you pat him gently, make noises and faces at him, and mimic his noises. Most preschoolers love making weird faces and noises, and the baby is a superb audience for their antics. Babies begin to watch their siblings with rapt fascination during their third month. By seven or eight months, many babies find their older siblings more amusing than anyone else in the family.

Your first child will copy you, of course, in many of the ways you try to capture and hold the baby's attention, but notice how he also begins to introduce his own versions of your strategies. Even if they have trouble managing games like peek-a-boo, which depend on delicate timing, preschoolers can do great song-and-dance routines (song-and-jump routines, really) that transfix the baby with delight.

You can encourage these entertainments in lots of ways. Point out the baby's interest and response, for example—"She's watching you!" "Ooh, she likes it when you do that!" And praise your firstborn for doing such a good job of entertaining the baby. Interpret the baby's reactions for the older child; it won't do any harm to exaggerate the delight of the baby in his older sibling ("He *does* like you so!"). If the baby seems overwhelmed, suggest variations on the older child's performance. "Perhaps she'd enjoy a quiet song now, how about that rock-a-bye one, can you *whisper* it?"

One of the great pleasures as the months go by is seeing the baby's growing delight in his older sibling. Increasingly, they laugh at their antics, enthralled. "She thinks he's marvelous," said one mother of her eight-month-old daughter and older son. "Hero-worships him. If he plays with her foot, she kills herself laughing. She doesn't cry till he goes out of the room." Another mother noted her daughter, also eight months, misses her brother when he isn't around. "She shouts till she hears him in the morning. Fusses till she sees him. I'm not enough." Interestingly, in both these families the older child was not especially warm or friendly to the baby.

All this adoration is great for your older child. And it is something that you can ruthlessly play on in dealing with the green-eyed monster of jealousy. By ten to twelve months many babies miss their older siblings when they are gone, and greet them with special delight when they return. Don't hesitate to point all of this out to your firstborn. "She's so pleased to see you! Oh, she thinks you're great!" "Look how you can make him laugh!" "You can *really* cheer him up!"

THEIR FIRST CONVERSATIONS

By two to three months your baby is likely to be making a range of odd noises and coos, and these soon expand to a repertoire of laughs, squeaks, and growls. These funny noises often delight older siblings, who mimic them with glee. This imitation often leads to a "reply" from the baby. Try suggesting to your firstborn that he mimic the baby's noises if this hasn't occurred to him—and see how the baby enjoys it.

Even children who are barely two years old talk to babies in "baby talk," just as adults do. They will speak in a high voice, ask and repeat lots of questions, and make the pattern of their speech go up and down in an exaggerated way. And they will try to hold their sibling's attention by saying his name—or addressing him as "Baby!" "Hi, Susie! Hi, Susie! What do you want? Do you like my funny hat-hat? Boo-boo-boo to you-you-you!" If you eavesdrop on your older child talking to her baby sibling, you'll hear how this "baby talk" changes over the months as the older one gets more skilled at holding the baby's attention and the baby becomes more responsive. Their "conversations" gradually get longer and longer. Probably children pick up some of this "baby-talk" technique from hearing you talk to the baby—but mostly it develops simply from the older child's interest in holding the baby's attention and eliciting the reward of that response.

SOOTHING AND CALMING

Most older children are concerned when their baby sister or brother is crying or upset, and many will do their best to soothe the little one. A preschooler will try out things he's seen you do when the baby is distressed—talking, patting, giving a pacifier, distracting with toys. You can help by showing what you think works best at this particular stage.

More annoying, your oldest is also likely to show concern if you have just scolded the baby! To many mothers it can seem like "conspiracy": "If I tell the baby off, he says 'Oh, you are mean. She doesn't understand' and he goes and cuddles her. Or he reprimands me—'You mustn't do that to Becky, she's only a baby.' "

If your firstborn's attempts to stop the baby crying don't work, he may get very frustrated and "turned off." It's good to keep an eye out for such moments, and to intervene to help if it's getting too frustrating for *either* of your children!

AMBIVALENCE

Even though your firstborn child shows concern about the baby's distress, he sometimes also deliberately tries to *increase* his baby sibling's upset, or becomes gleeful at his distress.

I watched three-year-old Laura caress her baby brother to try to calm him by saying: "All right, baby!" Then she turned to her mother and said, "Smack him!"

Two-year-old Cheryl kissed her baby sister saying: "Sister! Sister!" But to her mother she said, "Monster! Monster!"

Such ambivalence is extremely common. As the babies grow up, they become, of course, very adorable, smiling at everyone, and cooing at anyone who glances their way. You may notice that your previously amiable firstborn "turns" on the baby at precisely those moments when she is charming everyone in sight. He may suddenly suggest that you get rid of the baby, or announce "I don't like her" or "I wish she wasn't here." "We've had Henry long enough" was one four-year-old's comment when baby Henry was a particularly delightful and sociable five-month-old.

You may notice at this point your firstborn administering one of those hugs that continues even when the baby begins to cry or a cuddle that gets a bit too tight. If so, point out that he is hurting his sister, and find him something else to do that interests him, saying firmly, "That *hurts* her. She isn't enjoying that, it's too tight. Let's leave her in peace."

You may hear lots of verbal insults directed at the baby from your four- to six-year-old firstborn. Some may be pretty simple: "Fatty!" "Silly crybaby!" Others may be more inventive—and even scatological! And you may well overhear, "I *hate* you!" when your older one is really angry. It's hard to sit idly by at moments like these. Point out that the second born's feelings can be hurt, but try not to come down hard on your firstborn. It is good for him to feel able to express his hurt and jealousy. If you can turn "naming" into a joke, the tension will be eased. Make a joke about your *own* name, for instance.

Yet frequently the children who occasionally squeeze too hard or pester the baby to crying point, or who make negative remarks, show the most genuine affection and concern for the baby. Remember that a few negative remarks *aren't* a sign of wholesale rejection. Consider them in the context of all the positive things your older one does too—the concern over crying, the attempts to entertain, the clumsy "conversations." As one exhausted mother commented, "It all comes down to love *and* hate, doesn't it!"

One way to minimize the jealousy your firstborn feels is to point out similarities between him and his sibling. Remind him of what he was like when he was a baby. If you have videotapes and pictures of your firstborn at this stage, now is the time to bring them out. Tell him stories about what *he* did at three months, and what you used to do to soothe him. Fond family stories of his babyhood will reassure him that he is loved.

And make sure he's around and listening in when you tell the grandparents and the visitors that "It's Ian who she loves to be with and watch—Ian's her hero!" This is a great help in subduing jealousy. Knowing that he has a worshipful fan can heal the bruised confidence of a displaced firstborn. You can make it part of the family "lore" that she adores him. Pretty soon it'll be part of his sense of who he is—a loved older brother.

Finally, you may find it useful to show your firstborn one of the commercial videotapes made for children with new siblings. A good one is *Hey, What About Me?* made by Kidvidz (available from 618 Centre Street, Newton, MA 02158) in which no adults appear. It shows a series of young children interacting with their baby siblings—mimicking them and having the kind of "conversations" we've described in this chapter, trying to soothe or feed them, and talking about their mixed feelings about the baby and all the attention he or she gets. The kids even talk about some of the ways they cope with feeling blue (going out to play with a friend, telling their parents how they feel, for example). This video is great for kids between five and six.

GAMES BEGIN ...

By eight to ten months you may well notice your baby beginning to join in games with his older sibling—especially if he's lucky enough to have a *very* patient older sister or brother. By the end of the first year and early in the second, your two will probably have some games they've developed together—games that inevitably lead to wild laughter. Sometimes these games are very simple indeed. A typical example: Sally, a boisterous three-year-old bouncing up and down on the settee, catches the eye of eighteen-month-old Barry. Barry laughs, and scrambles up to join her, and he starts to bounce too. Both bounce together, shrieking with laughter. When their mother, Lizzy comes in full of concern for her settee, the laughter and bouncing get even wilder. Lizzy comments: "It's a stage of collusion and conspiracy—against me!" Chasing games, hide-and-seek, rolling, giggling together, all start to happen in that second year.

A particularly long-suffering older sibling will participate in even more elaborate games. I have seen eighteen-month- and twenty-four-month-old younger sisters playing soccer (though they were prone to wander off with the goalposts). I've also often seen younger siblings initiated into make-believe games, instructed on how to "be" schoolchildren, bus passengers, babies (of course), astronauts on rockets to the moon, birthday party guests, "Daddy," and so on. It is paradise for second children to be welcomed into the older one's world of pretend in this way—far more exciting than anything their parents can provide in the way of entertainment. They watch and imitate their adored older siblings with close attention. It is also wonderful for parents to watch this happening—one of the joys of having two that makes all the other, harder stuff seem worthwhile.

SUMMARY OF TIPS TO HELP THEM ENJOY EACH OTHER:

- *Encourage "conversation."*
  Encourage your siblings to communicate by getting the older one to imitate the coos and squeaks.

- *Offer praise.*
Praise your firstborn—enthusiastically—when he shows affection and interest in the baby.
- *Highlight the baby's interest in your firstborn.*
Draw your older child's attention to (and even exaggerate!) any signs of the baby's interest in him.
- *Explain the baby's feelings and actions.*
Interpret the baby's behavior for the older one in a very positive way: "He's looking at you—he likes you!"
- *Point out similarities between them.*
Tell the older child whenever the occasion arises: "He's doing it just the way you did when you were little!"
- *Let him try to soothe and comfort.*
Praise him lavishly when he succeeds in calming the baby!
- *Use videotapes of young brothers and sisters.*
Show him tapes of *himself* as a baby. Try out the various commercially available videotapes.

PART TWO

Conflict
and Rivalry

Chapter 8

COMPETITION, RIVALRY, AND CONFLICT

U p to now, we have looked at the problems and pleasures of siblings in the first two years. This next section of the book focuses on a set of issues that last a lifetime: competition, rivalry, and the conflicts that are so common among brothers and sisters. The intensity of sibling fighting and arguing—not just in the early childhood years but throughout the school years too—takes many parents by surprise. It destroys our idyllic fantasy of blissful family life. As the years pass, we confront not just the upset of our first-born child, but also a complex relationship between *two* children, both of whom often feel competitive and angry and let those feelings be known uninhibitedly. Parents often feel their children's fighting reflects some failure on their part. And few of them realize that the same thing goes on in other families. But it does. As Tina, mother of three-year-old Steve and five-year-old Evan, says: "Every minute of the day they're at it—arguing and fighting. I used to think I'd like lots of kids—but I couldn't take any more of this! It's often over the silliest things . . . why on earth do they do it?"

Why *do* Tina's two boys argue so much? And what can parents do in the face of endless arguments between their children? These are questions I'll be exploring in the pages that follow.

RIVALRY: A FACT TO BE LIVED WITH

Rivalry and competitiveness between siblings is extremely common. It is also perfectly natural and understandable—in fact, it is more unusual when children *don't* argue with each other. In most families there are frequent arguments, so you need not feel that it is because of some special failing on your part that your children endlessly squabble.

But even when you understand that rivalry is common, chances are that you will still feel upset and fed up with the endless arguing, and especially the physical aggression. Conflict between siblings is very hard for any parent to take. Even if you experienced it quite a bit yourself as a child, you often forget just how intense or frequent those fights were. Sibling battles can be particularly upsetting for parents who were only children and never experienced them first hand. As Cora put it:

> I take my kids' fights so much to heart—I'm horrified when they go for each other. I hate physical violence in any

form, and to see my own two trying to hurt each other is *awful*. I just wasn't prepared for it—no one ever yelled at anyone in my own family, let alone hit each other. I had no brothers and sisters to quarrel with. My husband was one of four kids, and he just laughs about our own two quarreling—says they're doing fine. He gets along so well with his brothers now, and yet he says they fought all the time as kids.

Unfortunately rivalry and competitiveness between siblings are not usually short-lived reactions to the arrival of a new sibling. Even though the immediate signs of a firstborn's unhappiness—the sleeping problems and toilet-training breakdown discussed above—disappear in time, the basic feelings of displacement don't. In fact, his jealousy is likely to intensify, and your second child will have fierce competitive emotions of her own. Rivalry *lasts*. Listen to adolescent siblings, or even adult brothers and sisters (maybe you and your own siblings!). It may have gone underground, but just scratch the surface and old rivalries show up, especially at times of family crisis.

Much of the fighting has to do with both your children's feelings about their place in the family sun—that is, their place in both their parents' love, affection, respect, approval. In each family, the rivalry is expressed in different ways—and the preferred method and style of fighting will change as the years pass. Here are some real-life situations of sibling conflict:

Andy, aged 2½ years, and Susie, 14 months
   Andy is a shy, rather anxious and sensitive child. His sister Susie is a boisterous, bouncy, and confident girl, clearly adored by her mother. On this particular day Susie had persistently tried to get something she'd been repeatedly for-

bidden by her mother. Finally Susie triumphantly achieved her goal, and her mother commented with exasperated pride and warmth in her voice:

"Susie, you *are* a determined little devil!"

Andy, watching the exchange from the other side of the room, commented sadly to his mother:

"*I'm* not a determined little devil." At this, his mother, laughing, said in an offhand tone:

"No, you're not! What are you? A poor old boy!"

Although Andy is only two and a half, he's already noticing his mother's different response to Susie and is comparing himself with his sister. What's more, he has picked up his mother's pride in Susie's persistence.

Of course, firstborns are not the only ones who feel jealous. You may well notice your second-born two-year-old demanding attention, or wailing for your help, *just* as you are settling down to do something with his older sibling. Many second-born children get that timing very well worked out in their second and third years, shrewdly using their new powers of talking, joking, and playing to shift the spotlight from older brothers and sisters to themselves. Polly, a particularly charming two-year-old in one of our studies, became increasingly adept at getting her parents' attention away from her older sister, Joanne. When any games began between Joanne and her parents, she tried to intervene, to draw attention to *herself*. Her efforts became more sophisticated month by month. At twenty-four months, when her mom was joining Joanne in playing a pretend game in which Joanne took her dolls to school, Polly simply charged into the conversation, insistently ordering her mom to "look at *my* doll!" By two and a half her interventions became more subtle. One day she managed to join in the pretend game of shopping that Joanne and

Mom were playing by cleverly deflecting the game to go *her* way. "My shop's got bananas for you! Come get my bananas!" Rather than reprimand Polly for interfering or gently persuade her to enter into Joanne's game, their mother turned her attention to buying Polly's bananas. Joanne was understandably upset. In another incident Polly kept pursuing her sister whatever she did, and finally Joanne screamed at her in fury. Their annoyed mother spoke crossly to Joanne, as Polly happily climbed onto her mother's knee. Joanne had been outmaneuvered by her younger sister, though this time her mother did not see it. This was a setup for explosive sibling rivalry.

In other families, conflict erupts when younger siblings bitterly resent the achievements of their older brothers and sisters, which seem to attract so much attention and delight from parents. Some preschoolers become upset when their older siblings start school. This was the case with Benjie. In the morning, Benjie stood around, feeling sullen and ignored, while everyone fussed about his older brother Jonny going off to school; then in the afternoon there was all the more excitement and talk about what he'd been doing at school. Their mother found she suddenly had to find ways of reassuring Benjie that he too was special. Patterns of rivalry change as both kids grow up and face new experiences and challenges.

WHY THEY FIGHT

Personality Clashes

If siblings feel irritated or hostile or jealous, they all too often express that hostility without inhibition. This is *not* always directly related to rivalry for parental love. There are plenty of other reasons that siblings dislike or resent each other. It may, for instance, be more a matter of clashing personalities than competition for Dad's attention. Siblings do not choose to live together; they are stuck with one another, day in day out. Close familiarity and enforced intimacy with another child brings plenty of tensions and friction, quite apart from the rivalry that your children may feel for your love and approbation. When their interests and styles clash—that's when trouble most often arises. In fact, in our research on brothers and sisters, we found that quarrels between siblings are most frequent in those families in which the personalities of the children differ markedly. Siblings who were like oil and water really did not mix happily!

Boredom

Some children provoke each other and fight because it livens up the boring family scene. When you've successfully provoked your sister, she may retaliate and then, best of all, *she'll* get into trouble with Mom and Dad. One mother, a professional psychologist who researches why kids become aggressive, believes that the conflict between her own children often begins because her lively, restless firstborn provokes his younger brother "just to stir things up a bit." When she's happily occupied, or something exciting is happening at home, she's far less likely to do this. We take their fighting seriously, but for the kids it's just another activity.

Possessions

Children under five are simply not good at sharing things. Their possessions are very much part of *themselves*. They also are not very tolerant. Learning to live and let live comes (we hope and pray) with the years. In most cases, the obsession with possessions starts to wane when children reach their fourth year. How much of an issue sharing is, then, depends a lot on how old your children are. In their book, *He Hit Me First*, Louise Bates Ames, distinguished child psychologist from the Gesell Institute, and her granddaughter, Carol Chase Haber, describe the impossibility of getting two-and-a-half-year-olds to share:

> The typical two-and-a-half-year-old wants complete possession of any object he is playing with, has played with, or might play with. While this madness is at its height, there is really very little that one can do about it. We once observed two-and-a-half-year-old Tommy in his playroom—his cart filled with all the toys it could hold, his arms and legs outflung protecting as many other objects as he could pile on the floor beside his cart. Whenever his young brother Doug attempted to touch anything either within Tommy's physical range or even in other parts of the room, Tommy would cry out angrily, "Mine!" (He of course couldn't play with *any* of these things because he was so busy protecting them.)

If Tommy and Doug were my children, I might have said something along the lines of: "What else could Dougie use?" or "Pretty soon it will be Dougie's turn," or "But Dougie *needs* it." Any of these may, with luck, be effective, as Louise Bates Ames points out. But if you have a two-and-a-half-year-old, getting him to share is especially hard. They *need* everything in sight—right away.

Territory, Space, and Rules

Related to arguments over possessions are arguments over space. One sibling will often complain about the other *being in his way*: sitting where he was sitting, going in his room, getting too close, touching his things, even—what a sin—looking at his picture.

Having a younger sibling hanging around when he is with his friends can be infuriating for an older sib. And, as with possessions, there are rules and privileges in every family that inevitably seem unequal and unfair to *someone* in the household. "Why should I have to help when he doesn't?" "His bedroom's worse than mine, why should I have to clean up?"

Control

Many sibling battles break out over seemingly trivial issues. You know the scenarios all too well: "*I* want to go in the front seat of the car!" "He got the cookie I wanted!" "I want to watch the *other* TV program." "He always gets to have the cup with Santa on—and I don't!" Winning these battles is not just about sitting in the front seat of the car, or getting the cookie or TV program you want. It's about asserting yourself and being in control, and that's far from a trivial matter in childhood. It is often the second born who makes these complaints, usually when he's feeling like the little one in the bottom of the family pile.

Fatigue and Hunger

And, of course, as every parent knows, tiredness, hunger, and illness are also high on the list of reasons siblings quarrel. If you are tired and cross, whom do you take it out on? Your brothers and sisters. Children argue more with their siblings when they are tired and right before meals—just as husbands and wives do.

There is no single answer to the question "Why do they quarrel?" There are layers and layers of reasons. First, there's the immediate cause—"He's taken my book"; then there's the struggle for control, power, status—the David and Goliath battle; then there's the deep-down and years-in-the-making jealousy over parental attention and love. Your kids could be quarreling about issues at any one of these levels, or indeed at all of them. It's worth taking a moment to see if you can figure out the primary reasons they argue. Understanding the background motivation behind the conflict can help you find a resolution.

SIBLING ARGUMENTS DON'T MEAN THERE'LL BE AGGRESSION OUTSIDE THE FAMILY

One encouraging finding that stands out from the research on sibling quarrels is that a child who gets into fights *within* the family does not necessarily behave aggressively outside the family. If your child is endlessly competitive and jealous of his sibling, and seems to care little about hurting her feelings, it does *not* mean that he's growing up to be an inconsiderate, hurtful person toward his friends or others outside the family. The family, which is the primary source of warmth and security for children, is also the arena in which they can express their feelings most freely. Where siblings are concerned, it's often a no-holds-barred expression. Some of the children who are fiercest in their competitiveness and hostility to their siblings have the closest friends outside the family: They are often the very excitable, sociable children who are fun for other kids to play with. They may be quite quarrelsome, but that doesn't stand in the way of their friendships.

But this does not mean that you have to sit by and witness his battles at home without comment. Your role is to teach him that you care about people being considerate and kind *inside* the family as well as outside. Being out of control emotionally is frightening for your child; you'll be helping him if you can steer him through those moments of intense rivalry and competition without an explosion.

THE FIGHTS GET FEWER OVER TIME

Research also shows that fighting does decrease over time (too slowly, it may seem to you) so there is light at the end of the tunnel. The peak is usually when your children are under five. By the time they are both at school, they have a wider world of friends and activities and more distractions from each other. They also learn—eventually—to resolve some of their disputes more equably. And they become better able to control their impulse to tear into each other.

Even more good news is that siblings who quarrel a lot and are very competitive are often quite friendly and cooperative in other ways. When they are not fighting and arguing, these sibling pairs play great games together and enjoy each other's company. Could it be that they are learning through the competitive arguments— learning something that helps them manage to play together?

CONSTRUCTIVE COMPETITION

Competitive behavior takes many forms, many of which are strongly approved of in our culture. Parents urge their kids to compete hard in sports, and in tests at school. They praise them with delight when they win competitions. Competitive sports draw huge crowds and are watched avidly on TV; people passionately follow the successes and failures of "their" teams, or "their" sporting heroes and heroines. And we encourage our children to compete with themselves as well as with others—to strive to beat their own usual achievements. We *approve* of competition in so many situations. Our children learn that fast.

And comparing ourselves with other people is not only part of our particular culture, it's an important part of human learning and interaction. Children begin to compare themselves with others—especially with their siblings—at an astonishingly early age. Remember Andy, on page 127? At two and a half years he was comparing himself unfavorably with his sister—sadly. When kids play together, whether preschoolers or older, they compete intensely over who will do what, over who's the best or most appropriate to take the lead role. Even two children doing something as innocent as making cookies will vie with each other over who has made the best, the biggest or smallest, the funniest, the weirdest. Sometimes it seems as if their whole orientation to the world and themselves is a competitive one.

The energy of that competitive drive can of course help your child to excel, and he will get pleasure from his achievements. It is one way that he can develop a sense of self-confidence, though it is certainly not the only way. Parents can foster this kind of healthy competition, but we should be careful not to overdo it. The ideal is to encourage each one of our children to develop his or her own special talents. Take care, however, not to dwell too exclusively on those achievements. It's great to give support, but not if a child feels that we value him only for his achievements. And don't *encourage* competition between siblings—it happens naturally enough anyway.

Second, children have to learn to lose; they can't always be the star. Learning to live with disappointment without getting very upset, and learning to cope with being less than a success are clearly very important achievements. But this doesn't come easily, especially when it is a sibling who is the victor. Your calm and cheerful support of your child's losses will be greatly needed. In some families one particular child always seems to be on the losing end, and it is painful for a parent to watch that child's frustration and disappointment. As he grows up, he becomes more and more conscious that he's not the successful one in the family, and he can increasingly become upset about his failures. You can really help by showing him his strengths, and bolstering his shaky confidence. Encourage him to spend time with his friends or to pursue his own sports activities or hobbies. All of these can help him develop a sense of identity and confidence—away from that frequently annoying sibling who is so adept at grabbing attention from him.

LEARNING ABOUT OTHER PEOPLE

Kids also begin to learn how to sort out their day-to-day disagreements through arguments. It is the forum in which they learn how to negotiate, conciliate, reach a compromise solution. To the poor harassed mother listening to the repetitions of "It's my turn!" "No it's my turn!" it may seem as if her children do nothing but squabble. But these arguments can teach them a lot, even if they don't concede with grace. At the very least, they are learning about someone else's point of view, and eventually they learn that they'll have to take that point of view into account. They are learning, too, about what upsets and annoys the other, and what will cheer him up. Of course, that's knowledge they can use for good or evil—and you can be sure that it won't all be for good with most brothers and sisters. But as a parent, one of your tasks is to maximize the good. You can begin to do this even with young children by identifying the seeds of compromise and helping them to grow.

WAYS TO DECREASE CONFLICT

Everyone in the family would be happier, of course, if there was less conflict between the kids. Here are some ideas of what you can do (or avoid doing) to make your family life more harmonious:

Avoid labeling and comparing. "She's always the one who . . ." "the anxious one . . ." "the athlete . . ." Sometimes these labels sound very positive to us, but our kids may not hear it this way. And the other children may feel slighted in comparison. You may be feeling affectionate when you label one child the family clown, the klutz, the slob, the sleepyhead, the space case—but the label may stick, at least in the child's mind. And in his sibling's mind too: As he grows older, his sibling will be unmerciful in the use of the label, drawing attention to each clumsy or clownish or sloppy act.

If you notice the teasing and name-calling, try to do two things. First, take the other sibling aside and point out that it's hurtful and unfair to keep referring to that trait. Second, make sure to praise and reassure the labeled child for positive things he does. He will need all the reassurance he can get to counterbalance the powerful and relentless sibling assault and mockery.

Remember, too, that if you are modeling this behavior, you'll be sending a conflicting message. Most parents understand that it's not a good idea to compare their children—at least in front of them—but it is difficult not to do this. If one child is helpful and cooperative and obliging, and the other never helps, it's hard not to point that out to the one who never raises a finger. One mother of two commented on how she came home from work exhausted most days, and her younger daughter would very often come and help with the cooking, or set the table, without being asked. They had a good chat, and it became a nice routine for the two of them. The older daughter never did a thing to help, and, of course, her mother complained to her, inevitably pointing out the virtues of her sister. The comparison cannot have helped—indeed the firstborn complained that her mother *clearly* preferred her sister "because she always wheedles her way into favor." Her mother gradually realized that she'd have to find moments when the younger sister wasn't around to encourage her disgruntled firstborn to help.

Comparisons about looks, success at school, achievements, or talents should be avoided at all cost. It is bad enough when visitors or relatives comment, "You've got a smart sister, haven't you!" "When are you going to be a baseball star like your brother?" Even the comment "He has the looks of your side of the family, while she has our family's brains" can be interpreted as an insult by one—or both—children. If your children are still at the preschool and early childhood stage, you may think all this is irrelevant. But it's not: Children pick up these family "mythologies" about who they are, what their special qualities are, and what their foibles are, very early. I heard mothers with firstborn preschoolers and second-born babies make these remarks while their older child listened: "Oh, Harry's such an easy baby—if I'd had another like Penny was, I'd be in the hospital!" "They're as different as night and day. I could put him down, and he'd just wait to be fed. Now *she's* so full of life and on the go, she keeps me jumping!" Just remember, your preschooler picks up these things very fast indeed, and notices the warmth in your tone as you describe her sibling!

Siblings also pick up on those proud glances that you exchange with your husband when you're both delighted by *one* of your children's clever remarks. It's all fuel for jealousy. Of course it is great to notice your child's achievements, but remember to keep the balance by praising things in *both* children.

Shield younger siblings from no-win situations. If your younger child is sadly conscious that he's not as strong or effective as his older brother, you can point out to him that he *will* be taller, bigger, and stronger when he's older, and able to do all the things he now sees the older kids doing. Just as we saw that kids love stories about themselves as babies, they also love to hear stories about what *will* happen to them as they grow older. You can put those two stories together: "When you were little, last year, we went to Granny's, and you were so small, you rode on my back in the swimming pool, remember? This summer you're going to be big enough to go in the kids' pool there—and next year maybe you'll be a swimmer all on your own!" You can help younger siblings by keeping them out of competitive situations with those older siblings too.

Enlist the help of your older child. Younger brothers and sisters very often admire and try to imitate their older siblings, at least in the early years. If you can persuade your older to help your younger to learn to build things, throw a ball, or climb, *both* kids feel good about themselves (at least until the harmony disintegrates into willful pupil and impatient teacher—then call an end to it!). When six-year-old Joanne had got into a rut of fighting over the new swing set with her four-year-old sister, their dad got the idea of asking Polly to show Joanne how to pump. Joanne was proud of her superior skill, and Polly was rapt for a good five minutes. Doing things together is what makes the attachment between them grow; and it also helps to build your oldest's confidence in herself.

Protect your older child. If your eager toddler always tries to join in your firstborn's games—alone or with his friends—you may have to protect your older child. It is unfair to the firstborn if every time she sets up her pretend games or her precious things, along he comes and cheerfully grabs. It is great to tell her that "He's too small to understand that he's spoiling it," but this is not enough. Make sure the older child gets privacy to play by taking the toddler off to the kitchen with you. Try to anticipate those invasions; whisk him off before he wrecks the game and the screams of outrage rock the neighborhood.

Set rules and limits. Parents differ in how strongly they feel about yelling, swearing, or teasing between siblings, and in how much they care about politeness and consideration for others (even siblings). Some *want* their children to "stand up for themselves" if their "rights" are at issue. Others place a high premium on politeness and sharing. When issues crop up during your children's quarrels, decide which you consider *really* important. That way, your "message" to your children about whether this has to stop will come through clearly and consistently. Most important: Talk to your spouse about the issue, and work out your views together. If parents don't agree on what's allowable and what's not, kids pick it up very fast indeed, and exploit it. And remember, whatever your views on politeness, stick to the no-hitting rule!

Rick, father of a five- and four-year-old, knew exactly which issues he felt strongly about:

> The clearest rule is *no hitting*. Whoever started it, hitting is out! No exceptions. Deliberately destroying the other kid's things is out too. We discourage unkind name-calling—but that of course is difficult to draw a line about, because

sometimes it's *funny* . . . and doesn't hurt feelings. Then there's sharing—but I don't expect them to do that all the time—so of course they don't! But taking turns is something they've had drummed into them, and they take that seriously.

When you establish rules, remember to make them simple and concrete. Vague general admonishments to "Be nice!" "Play nicely!" will have no effect. "No hitting in this house" is more likely to register. And be sure to direct them to *both* kids. "You *two* can sort this thing out outside." "You *two* can take turns over that."

Sharing. Learning to share is important, but it is also important to every child to have some possessions of his own, things that really become part of his growing sense of *who I am.* How difficult sharing is for your kids depends quite a bit on their age. Children between eighteen months and three find sharing especially hard. Don't force it on your eighteen-month-old.

If your kids are close in age and resent sharing things with each other, you might want to try to get duplicates when you buy them small things. I learned the hard way with my twins: After being away from them overnight, I spent hours choosing two *different* toy cars as presents for them on my return, and then found that the fact that they were different cars precipitated trouble. If your children are of the opposite sex, it makes it easier. You are less likely to have a boy yearning for his sister's possessions, or a daughter dying for her brother's toys.

Creating a special space for each of your children to keep his *own* possessions is a good idea, especially if they share a room. It can be very small—a box, particular drawers in a chest—but it all helps to give each child a sense of his or her special place, and (you hope) a sense of responsibility.

You can encourage preschoolers to share by making it something *they* decide about: "Here, we've got one big set of these for all of you. How can it be shared between you?" When sharing happens (and it often does, with cookies and candy, at least) be sure to reinforce it with praise. You can also point out the advantages of sharing: "If you both use the blocks together you can make a *huge* castle for all the knights!"

But don't lose heart if this doesn't work! Sharing still doesn't come naturally to most young kids.

Reward what you want to see them do. Support their cooperation; praise their signs of concern for the other child and their spontaneous sharing.

Don't impose your own past on the situation. "She's just like I was as a kid, and I don't want her to have to put up with what I got from my older brother!"

Try not to judge what's happening between your children in terms of what happened to you as a kid. It is your own child's individuality and sense of self that is important. So it doesn't help your children if you "see" what is happening between them in terms of your own former battles with a bullying brother and an overbearing sister. Of course there may be some similarities, but your daughter is herself—not a version of you as a child, and your son is not a version of your older brother.

IF YOU STEP IN . . .

Fighting is very hard on your nerves—as well as on the child who is losing the battle. But, though you may be sorely tempted to intervene, there are some good reasons to stay out of their verbal quarrels. Even with the most skilled detective work you probably won't find out who is to "blame" because sibling quarrels have such long and tangled roots. Your involvement increases the hope of both kids that you will take their side, and thus your intervention actually may encourage more quarreling. If you settle their arguments for them, they don't learn to sort things out for themselves.

But you can assist in the process by getting them to *talk* to each other about the problem when they seem to be losing control, and encouraging each one to try to see the other's point of view. Ask each child how he would feel if that teasing or name-calling or toy-grabbing had been done to *him*. Remember that in the end you aren't doing your child a favor by teaching him he needs you to rescue him from trouble with his sibling.

Some discourage parental intervention on the grounds that it rewards the children for quarreling. But this is less convincing to me. The assumption here is that they mainly argue in order to get your attention, but this is by no means always the case once they are beyond the first months of having a sibling.

While it is best to keep out of their arguments as much as you can, staying out is often easier said than done. And when parents find themselves intervening despite their best efforts not to, they end up feeling that they're failing at this impossible job of bringing up happy kids. Clearly there are lots of situations when you *can't* stay out of it: in the case of physical violence (see next chapter) or when there is real verbal assault and battery, when the tension level is excruciating, or when one or both have lost control and they obviously cannot get out of the spiral of hostility on their own. And expecting kids always to "work it out" by themselves can mean turning a blind eye to bullying and teasing that causes real distress (see Chapter Nine).

When you do intervene, *do it to help the children understand and communicate with each other*, and to encourage them to learn to deal with each other on their own. Here are some tips to bear in mind:

- Listen to both children's position, not just one—even if there's apparently a clear "victim." Keep your comments neutral, responses like "Oh?" "Hmmm" "I see . . ." show you have registered the complaint but are not taking sides.

  Try to set the scene so *they'll* work it out, with a solution *that is fair to them both*. You could say: "You two need to solve this . . ." or "How are you two going to solve this?" or "What are you two going to come up with as a solution that will work for both of you?" If they can't work it out alone, separate them. But do so without blaming one or the other. You can say: 'You both will have to go to your rooms so you can stop your fighting," or "Since you can't get along right now, you'd better be apart for ten minutes . . ." If your second born is still a toddler, speak to her in the same way as you do your older child. Your firstborn will understand that you are not showing the younger one favoritism. If the two kids share a bedroom, put them in different parts of the house—for example, one in the kitchen and one in the living room. Of course, they won't like it, and you may find that this unites them against you . . . but at least they aren't quarreling, and they begin to feel like a team!
- In cases of extreme teasing you can use a "time-out." Here the

children are sent out of the room (to their rooms, to sit on the stairs, etc.) and told to stay there either until (a) a timer rings, or (b) they are "ready" to be reasonable, nonviolent, nice, or whatever. The timer works very well with lots of young kids. Even those who completely lose control and get wild with fury will usually calm down and wait (it's surprising, but common!), and the timer takes *you* out of the fight.

• Try out role-playing or role-reversal. Get your younger child to play the role of her older sibling in this argument and your older one to play the second born. Chances are the quarrel will dissolve in laughter—but each may also learn something about how the other feels. This can work surprisingly well with four- to six-year-olds who haven't gotten so upset that they've lost control.

• If one particular object always seems to lead to fights, remove it for a specified length of time (half an hour or longer) as soon as they have started fighting over it. If the fights resume, you may want to put it away for a while.

The general message is this: If you do intervene, *do it to help them understand and communicate with each other,* and to encourage them to begin to deal with each other on their own. If they refuse or cannot manage it, separate them.

TALK TO EACH KID ONE-ON-ONE

If you want to talk to your child about why she teases her sibling so often, do it when you're alone with her, not while her brother overhears and smirks at his sibling getting in "trouble." She's more likely to tell you what she's feeling when you are alone with her. And if she tells you she *hates* her brother, don't deny your child's feelings. Don't simply say, "Oh, no, you don't—he's your brother so you love him!" If she weren't upset about him, she wouldn't be talking to you about it. Try to find out *why* she gets so angry with him, and see if there are ways you can help.

TRY MAKING A CHART OF WHEN THE QUARRELS HAPPEN

If the frequency of the arguments is really getting to you, you could try making a list or diary of when the arguments occur and what they're about, as well as of the times the kids play happily together. You may discover that they are mostly doing very well together, which should cheer you up. It might also give you some sense of what precipitates most arguments and when they happen so you can take preventive action: If they argue most over the TV in the evenings, make sure one of them has some other interesting things to do at that time. If the fights come just before naptime or before meals, that suggests tiredness and hunger are increasing the tension. Ward off that hunger with healthful snacks, and try to make sure that they don't get too fatigued. This might be a good time to simply keep them apart.

IT'S NOT MOM'S FAULT

Children are often more compliant with their father than their mother—for a number of different reasons. They are more used to hearing their moms say no, they may have learned that Mom can be "gotten around" but Dad can't, they may associate Dad with fun and games because they see less of him, and so on. But if this is how things are in your family, *do not* let yourself be blamed by your spouse or your other relatives for being the "incompetent mother." Children quarrel for all the reasons we've discussed; the major reason that yours argue is *very* unlikely to be simply because you are an oversympathetic, permissive, incompetent mother. As Louise Ames Bates and Carol Chase Haber put it in their book *He Hit Me First*: "Children of all ages *take things out* on their mothers, behave with them much worse than they would dream of with others." And fathers who bring up their kids alone, or are very highly participant, have much the same kind of experience.

Sibling arguments can seem trivial and endless, and can be *very* irritating for parents. Some survival tips follow; most important of all, perhaps, is for you to keep a sense of humor—and to realize these quarrels will decrease. There *is* light at the end of the tunnel.

SUMMARY OF TIPS FOR PREVENTING AND REACTING TO VERBAL QUARRELS

- *Avoid comparing and labeling them.*
  It will only make things worse.
- *Protect your firstborn from too much invasion.*
  Give your firstborn some space and privacy, and watch out for the intrusions of the second born on your firstborn's activities.
- *Remove yourself.* If your children are in the five- to six-year range or older, go far away so you don't hear the squabbles.
- *Try to keep the children occupied.*
  So many quarrels begin because children are bored and restless: Keeping your kids actively involved and interested in things will keep the quarreling level low.
- *Keep them apart before the fights begin.*
  They may well be spending too much time on top of each other.

- *Praise their efforts to play together and cooperate.*
  If your second born is a toddler, help (as unobtrusively as possible) to support their joint games—with any luck you can fade out of this particular picture soon.
- *Keep out of verbal quarrels if you can.*
  If you try to act as the judge, it often promotes competition.
- *If you intervene, keep your intervention short and simple and nonpartisan.* Set the scene so *they* work out the solution; separate without blame.
- *Remember, things get better.*
  Don't forget that all this quarreling is normal, and not your fault, and that it will decrease in time. Meanwhile, maybe what you all need is less "togetherness," and more time apart. Plan an escape route for *yourself.*

Chapter 9

HITTING AND HURTING AS THE CHILDREN GROW UP

VIOLENCE IN FAMILIES

Do your children kick and hurt each other? They are not alone. Over half the children in one large-scale study in the U.S. did one of the following to their siblings in the course of a year: kicked, bit, punched, hit with object, beat up, attacked with knife or gun. The violence *does* decrease as the children grow up, but slowly: It's at its peak with three- to four-year-olds; however, it is still very common among five- to nine-year-olds. Ask your children about how they try to get their siblings to do what they want—and you are very likely to hear some disconcertingly violent strategies. Beating up, hitting, and teasing are high on the list. So if your children are violent, they aren't unusual. But while that may take some of the sense of special failure or responsibility off your shoulders, it doesn't make the violence any more acceptable.

The reasons that siblings assault each other change as they grow up. When Caitlin was three and her brother Kirk was a newborn, her physical aggression toward him was largely a comment on her relationship with her mother—an expression of her feelings of being excluded and unloved. By now, when Kirk, at age two, takes five-year-old Caitlin's favorite toys from her own private toy box and destroys the castle she had spent all morning building, she lashes out with fury aimed directly at him. Her relationship with her brother has its own shape and color, and the reasons for hitting that annoying brother have much more to do with her feelings about *him* as a person than with her anger at her mother. Of course, jealousy remains an issue at any age.

Other factors also loom large: In setting off an assault Caitlin's own mood, her tiredness, boredom, the effects of her day at preschool, how her mother responds to her behavior, all exacerbate her fury at Kirk's interference. Just the same things that make adults irritable to their families!

Here's another typical incident involving violence that Caitlin and Kirk's mother Ann described. This happened one day when Caitlin was five and Kirk an adorable twenty-four-month-old:

> She came home from school irritable and tired. I saw that and felt "Oh, no, she's in that mood again" . . . so I was irritated by her even before she'd done anything. He was playing happily—such a placid, happy boy. And she went

over and just pinched him hard, out of the blue. Of course he wailed, and I was furious—and jumped on her immediately. Then she waited till I was out of the room and teased and attacked him again.

This time Caitlin's irritability, together with her negative feelings about Kirk *and* her mother's reactions, led to an escalation of the trouble. Ann realized afterward that she had probably made things worse by jumping on Caitlin because of her irritable mood, and by showing fury after Caitlin provoked her brother. Looking back on this episode, she now says, "I think it's important to watch your *behavior*—what you actually do and say to them; to separate out what your feelings are from how you treat the two of them. When she came in, I should have given her more of a chance, and I should have tried to be equally positive with them both."

That's very hard to do, especially when Caitlin has just gone after her brother with absolutely no provocation. But Ann's point about keeping your feelings under control is a very good one.

KEEP YOUR ANGER OUT OF IT IF YOU CAN

Don't let your feelings lead you into an escalating cycle of anger and violent confrontation. When your kid has annoyed and hurt you by breaking the rule about hitting, you're particularly likely to become especially hard on him. And if he picks that up, then he's likely to turn on you and get even more defiant.

But still the rule of NO VIOLENCE must apply to the entire family. Time-out, withdrawal of privileges or treats—the consequences of violence have to be negative and firmly held to. But remember, most important of all is that there should be *no violence from parents*. You are the most important models here.

CHANGING STRATEGIES AS KIDS GROW UP

Ann noticed that in those early months when Caitlin's violence to Kirk had to do with her anger toward her parents, time-out was a useful strategy. "Time-out worked initially because she was hurting him to get at us," she comments, "and with time-out there was no argument—she was just away from everyone."

But as the source of the conflict shifted to Kirk, time-out became less effective because it didn't give Caitlin's hostility any relief. This hostility had its roots in jealousy, but was often precipitated by his actions. Time-out simply delayed Caitlin's explosions.

What *does* lead to relief—and indeed to pleasure—is pinching, hitting, and hurting him. Children are quite frank about the pleasure they get from hurting their siblings. Caitlin tells her mother Ann "I just *want* to kick him!" for instance, and Ann is quite clear that Caitlin feels better after she's hurt Kirk. This is pretty disconcerting to hear, but the positive side—if your child makes such comments—is that at least you can talk about what is underlying those feelings.

TALK ABOUT HER FEELINGS

It can be a great help to talk to your older child about her feelings—and work out, together, what makes her violently angry with her sibling. It's not always easy to get an angry, sulky young child to talk, of course. Try to find a time when you're alone with her, when she's not overwhelmed with being upset.

REASSURE YOUR AGGRESSOR THAT HE IS STILL LOVED

Remind your wild and aggressive child at bedtime that he's loved, and lovely, and he is *not* going to hit his sister or beat up the cat tomorrow. Show him, too, that he has to use *words* to discharge those angry feelings, not fists.

TRY OUT OTHER STRATEGIES

Other parents have used these techniques to curb repeated hitting and hurting by their preschoolers, five- or-six-year-olds:

- Suggest that they draw pictures of each other—making them as ugly as they want . . . The idea is, they get a chance to express their anger in a way that doesn't physically hurt the other. Chances are the pictures will be so silly that they'll both end up laughing.
- Get them to role-play the scene they're fighting with their sibling about. This can help with quarreling children and when your children are physically fighting too.

DON'T REWARD THE AGGRESSOR

Remember not to pay special attention to the child who was hitting by taking her off with you. Even if you are simply telling her that it's wrong to hit, you're paying her more attention and abandoning (apparently) the victim. Instead, focus your attention on the victimized one. When Cheryl hits Stacey, say to Stacey, "Let me give that a rub and kiss—that looks sore. Cheryl needs to *say* what she's feeling, not to hit you."

SEPARATE THEM

Enforcing a cooling-off period with the warring parties in different rooms is the answer when the situation has really heated up. Hurtful actions have to be stopped. Half an hour of separation may do the trick.

APOLOGIZE OR NOT?

Some parents feel that they should make sure their firstborn children feel bad about what they've done and show that guilt by apologizing. While it is clearly important to teach kids a real sense of consideration for others and an awareness that their actions can hurt others, what parents get all too often when they insist on an immediate apology to a sibling is an even more furious and sulky kid muttering an obviously unfelt sentiment.

I feel that there are several problems with this approach. Forcing an apology makes children feel guilty without really understanding their role in the situation. In addition, it teaches the child to dissemble and disguise what he really feels. It is better to encourage him to talk to you about his real feelings, and for you both to deal with those together, than to push him into a lie.

BULLIES AND VICTIMS?

> Jake picks on *one* of his sisters—teases her unmercifully and pushes her around. She just whines and cries and comes to us, and somehow the way she reacts, so pathetically, just makes him worse.
>
> CRAIG, FATHER OF FIVE-YEAR-OLD JAKE

Does this sound familiar? Sibling conflict sometimes seems to fall into a vicious circle of bully and victim, in which one child is continually attacking another, who responds in an abject, passive way that seems to make the aggressor even more of a bully. But it is important not to fall into a habit of accusation and labeling yourself. Think carefully before you slot your children into those bully and victim roles.

First, you may not have all the information. Lots of adults admit *now* that they used to tease and needle their siblings until the other child lashed out and then was chastised by the parents as the bully. At the time, however, their parents saw only the last act of the drama—and so they misinterpreted what was really going on.

Second, it doesn't help your children's relationship to focus too much on the roles of bully and victim. When you keep up the refrains "Don't be such a bully!" "Oh, was he mean to you again, poor darling!" you are in fact assigning them these roles and making it harder for them to break out of them.

What can help (though it takes a lot of patience and humor on your part) is an idea recommended by Chaim Ginott in *Between Parent and Child*. Think of treating the kids as if they were *the kids you want them to become*. Instead of yelling at the aggressor, point out to him that he's good at persuading and talking, not pushing and shoving, and he *knows* he can be nice—so he'd better begin! Instead of saying "Stop being a bully, Scott!" try "No hitting, Scott, you *know* how to ask Katie to do it, and you *know* how to be kind too—start now!"

If immediately after your comment Katie calls Scott a mean bully, try to give her a better picture of her brother, which will also help him get a better view of himself: "Scott does know how to be friendly too. Try asking him instead of wailing—he can be generous too."

Instead of commiserating with the one who was hurt as "Poor thing!" show her that she's sturdier than she thought, and clever enough not to be picked on by her brother.

The fundamental idea is, *look after the child who's hurt or frightened without labeling and attacking the aggressor.*

SUMMARY OF DO'S AND DON'T'S ABOUT HITTING AND HURTING

- *Don't hit your children yourself.*
  Violence breeds violence, and you are a powerful model for your children.
- *Keep your emotions out of it.*
  As much as possible!
- *Separate them.*
  If they're hitting, hurting, biting, or punching each other, separate and isolate them.
- *Try time-out and role-play techniques.*
  Use *time-out* if they are preschoolers; try the role-play and draw-your-sibling techniques if they're older.
- *Pay attention to the victim, not the aggressor.*
  Don't abandon the victim and reward the aggressor with attention.
- *Reassure your wild one that he's loved.*

PART THREE

Siblings' Individuality

Chapter 10

WHY ARE THEY SO DIFFERENT FROM EACH OTHER?

When I went to get them from the party, there was Jay, the center of the whole gang—everyone always wants to play with him—and Aaron way off by himself, all shy and alone. This happens so often, it makes me wonder why *are* they so different? Is it just because Aaron's the first?

JON, FATHER OF SIX-YEAR-OLD AARON
AND FOUR-YEAR-OLD JAY

They really were very different, even as babies. My oldest was an easy baby—slept through the night very early, easy to feed. I thought being a mother was easy as pie. Then I had Gary—and oh, was that a hard time. He never slept, cried endlessly, so difficult to settle, always restless. But he was always *alert* too—looking around, seemed to need lots of distractions. Those differences were there right at the start.

CAROLINE, MOTHER OF FIVE-YEAR-OLD ARNOLD
AND THREE-YEAR-OLD GARY

Big differences between their children are noticed by most parents—differences in how easy they are as little babies, differences in personality as they grow up, in how easily they move into the world of school and friends outside the family, in how they handle difficulties and frustration. And the differences are there, strikingly, with adult brothers and sisters. (Think of yourself and your siblings, if you have them.)

Many parents are surprised by just *how* different their children are. Despite how different *we* are from our own siblings, we often expect our own children to be quite alike. After all, they are growing up in the same family—with the same parents, and the same family background and heredity. They live in the same house and neighborhood, have the same grandparents, take the same vacation trips, have the same books to read, TV to watch. So why does one child sit there quietly looking at books for hours, while the other runs around the house like a maniac, wildly swinging from one crazy game to the next? And why is one child so easy to handle, and the other one needs all the artful cunning her parents can summon to get her to do what they want? What made Jimmy Carter president of the United States, and his brother Billy a good ol' boy?

Behind such questions lurks a suspicion (and sometimes a worry) shared by many parents, that the children have turned out so differently because of how they are being raised.

On the other hand, many parents see the differences between their kids as a reassuring sign that many forces outside of them go into shaping their children's personalities. It is true that some of the differences between sisters and brothers are present from the start. Even within the same family babies have very different sleeping patterns and ways of feeding; they are different in how interested they are in looking around and in getting your attention. This was brought home to me dramatically with my fraternal twin boys: At birth they weighed exactly the same, but otherwise were so different—one wiry, strong, tense, always looking around, not easy to soothe, the other relaxed and easy going.

Research shows fairly conclusively that you need *not* feel solely responsible for those night-and-day differences between your children—there's a far more complicated story behind them.

WHAT CAUSES THEIR DIFFERENCES?

Heredity

"He's got your nose!" "She's just like her grandma—a real throwback to that side of the family!" "My mom has a special spot for my boy because he's so like my dad; she just doesn't feel the same way about my daughter."

Everyone is on the lookout for signs of connections with other members of the family when babies are born, and as they grow up. And we often describe the differences between brothers and sisters in terms of heredity: "She's just like me in that way, while the older one takes after her dad." Sometimes it's a matter for apprehension and suspicion—the idea that "bad blood" is turning up in one child in the family! Identical twins, of course, make the most striking example. And when identical twins have been separated at birth and brought up in different families, and then turn out to laugh the same way, walk the same way, gesture and talk the same way, choose the same professions—it is an eerie way of showing us just how important that shared heredity can be.

We look to heredity to explain the similarities between us and our children. The idea that something "runs in the family" is what genetics means to most people. Similarities between brothers and sisters also have a lot to do with heredity.

But there is another side to that coin. Each child inherits half his genetic makeup from his mother and half from his father, and as a result, on average, only half of what brothers and sisters inherit from their parents is in common. And that means that half of their inherited genetic makeup is *different* from their siblings.

Thus heredity *can also contribute to making them different.* So some of the differences we see between siblings are the result of genetic differences between them—they have nothing to do with their parents' preferences, or differences in the way they have been treated.

We might think that differences—like those of Jay and Aaron with whom this chapter begins—stem from the different way their parents handled their social lives—that Jay was taken to see other people more, and got used to meeting people, while Aaron had a more isolated early childhood—perhaps because his parents went out less, or lived a less social life when he was their only child. Surprisingly enough, shyness is one personality trait that is quite strongly influenced by genetics. If you compare identical twins, who are exactly the same in their genetic makeup, with fraternal twins, who are just like ordinary siblings who happened to be born at the same time, you find that identical twins are much more alike in the extent to which they are shy. Fraternal twins, on the other hand, run the full gamut of possibilities: They are no more likely to have the same level of shyness than any sibling pair.

Differences in activity are also influenced by heredity—at least by the time children are preschoolers and older. So if your first child at three was a dynamo and kept you on your toes, while your second one as a three-year-old is content to sit quietly and play for hours, then it is quite likely that these differences reflect genetic differences between them.

But differences in genetic makeup don't explain all the differences between your children. We can see this very clearly with identical twins who are exactly the same genetically yet whose personalities do differ in some ways. Differences between identical twins *cannot* be due to heredity, but must arise because of differences in their experiences.

Whatever the original sources of differences in their personality, these differences mean, of course, that everyone—grandparents, parents, siblings, friends, teachers at school—will relate to each of your children differently too. Differences in their "natures" are intricately bound up with differences in how they relate to others, and how others interact with them. From the beginning, then, their social worlds will be different. In this sense they do not grow up in the "same" family at all. And how you deal with some of the conflicts between them and how you manage their different lives *does* have an impact on the way they develop.

Different Lives within the Family

Brothers and sisters can have strikingly different experiences within the same family. The difference in their ages means everyone treats them differently. You might argue at length with your four-year-old (who is for the moment playing a princess) about whether it is reasonable to go out on the freezing porch in a ballet tutu and nothing else, and finally win with a compromise of tutu plus blanket-as-cloak. In contrast, when your one-year-old heads for the hot stove, you simply grab him. Traffic control with preschoolers and with toddlers is handled differently, obviously. And different parents just naturally have their own individual preferences for different ages or stages of child development. You might adore babies but find mutinous toddlers less wonderful. You might be impatient with the early months of infancy but charmed by your children as toddlers. For other parents, the pleasures of being with talkative, fantasizing preschoolers are best of all. Even if you love *all* the stages of childhood, you'll relate to your different-aged children differently. You may be cooing away blissfully with your little one, then have to deal with the *thousandth* request from your whiny preschooler—no wonder there's an edge of irritation in your voice. Or you may be (grimly) mopping up the food hurled to the floor by your ten-month-old for the third time in ten minutes, when your wonderful four-year-old comes in bursting with interesting things to tell you. Of course there are bound to be differences in how you respond to the two of them.

Children are very much aware of these differences, and if they feel much less loved than their siblings, it casts a long shadow. It is that sense of *relative* affection that makes a difference in the way they feel about themselves. In fact, recent research shows that kids are supersensitive to relative differences in their parents' attention and affection, so it is important to try very hard to minimize the differences in how you relate to them. This is far from easy. Your goal should be *appreciating* the specialness of each child. Here are some key pointers:

- Pay attention to each child's individual special needs, skills, and talents.
- Show each child he is loved *for himself*. If one child poses that bombshell question "Who do you love best?" tell him "Each of you is special. You're my wonderful boy—there's no one else who has your smile . . . or who thinks the way you do . . . you're my Tommy!" And find a moment to tell his sister how much you love *her* for herself too.
- Try to give them your attention and time *according to what they need*. If your second born comes and whines that you're spending too much time on his sister's homework, explain why his

sister needs you right now, that the homework is important for school (and he'll be doing it in a year too), that you know it is hard for him to wait, but that when his sister's homework is done, you'll do something special with *him*.

• Avoid comparing them! If one kid is untidy, don't say "why can't you be tidy like Sally?" Instead, try something like "that T-shirt looks great when it's not all crumpled—it'd be better on the chair." Listen to yourself talking to them, and when you're about to compare them (you're sure to catch yourself doing it) *stop yourself.*

Differences in How Your Children Treat Each Other Are Important

Another key influence on how each of your children develops is the way they treat each other.

Listen to how two siblings describe their relationship with each other. Nancy is ten, and her brother Carl is six. We asked them both about their sibling, and what they liked and disliked about each other. Here's how Nancy described Carl:

> Well, he's nice to me. And he sneaks into my bed at nighttime from Mommy. I think I'd be very lonely without Carl. I play with him a lot and he thinks up lots of ideas and it's very exciting. He comes and meets me at the gate after school and I think that's very friendly. He's very kind. Don't really know what I'd do without a brother.

Now here's how Carl describes Nancy:

> She's pretty disgusting and we don't talk to each other much. I don't really know much about her. There is nothing I really like about her. Sometimes when I do something wrong she tells me off. She's mean.

The differences in the way the two children describe this "same" relationship are striking. The sibling experience is very different for Nancy and for Carl—and this is true for very many brothers and sisters right from the earliest months. The different ways siblings experience their relationship can influence how each child feels about himself and his self-confidence. If one sibling is continually disparaged by her sibling but doesn't return the criticism, having a brother or sister can mean something different to each. Our studies have shown that children who receive this kind of criticism from their siblings without also feeling supported and liked by them tend to grow up more anxious, worried, and lacking in self-esteem. So siblings can have very different experiences within the same family. But, it's important to remember the differences in children's relationships with their siblings can change strikingly as children grow up. This kind of pattern can be a temporary glitch, not one that's set for a lifetime. (See Chapter Twelve).

Does Birth Order Matter?

Stories about the supreme importance of birth order in determining character abound. The idea that firstborns are more neurotic, more anxious, more eager to please their parents than later-born children is common currency. And you may have read about the "middle-child syndrome." But for the most part these beliefs about birth order just don't match up to reality. Careful research shows clearly that knowing someone's position in the family gives us very little power to predict what he is like, or how he will develop. Among all the influences on personality and well-being, birth order turns out to be relatively unimportant. Its influence is minor compared with genetics and social experiences that are not linked to birth order.

There are, however, clear links between birth order and how children behave with their siblings. These are just what common sense would lead us to expect: Firstborn children are usually more dominating and controlling over their younger siblings than vice versa, at least during the preschool years. Later-born children are probably more influenced by their firstborn siblings than vice versa: Sibling relationships are not symmetrical in those early years. For instance, second-born children imitate their older siblings quite a bit, while older siblings rarely model themselves on their younger siblings. How affectionate or hostile an older sibling has been to his younger brother or sister is likely to affect how that younger child behaves—but the reverse is less clearly so.

Firstborn children are likely to feel particularly discriminated against in terms of parental treatment: You'll probably hear more complaints that "It isn't fair!" from your oldest. And it is true that parents are frequently harder on their oldest kids. If there is a sibling quarrel, the oldest is more likely to get the blame—even though once the second born is over two years, he or she is just as likely to be the one who started the trouble. As parents, we should look out for this tendency to always blame that older kid.

Chance, Luck, and Personality

Finally, differences between siblings are also the result of individual life experiences that one child has—but the other misses. Biographies of famous people show us very clearly how important chance can be in influencing a child's development and personality. A serious illness sends one child to the hospital for a protracted period, a great teacher sets another child off on a new tangent at school, a chance encounter leads another child to discover that he loves play-acting—each occurrence can help a sibling to develop in a direction that is unique.

WHAT THIS MEANS FOR YOU

Once you understand that differences in your children's personalities are not only (or even mostly) due to how you have treated them, you can know that you aren't completely responsible for the way they grow and develop. Psychologist Sandra Scarr puts it this way: "As parents we tend to believe that we have enormous influences on our children. . . . Actually if we are reasonable, loving, but not perfect parents, children will grow up to be themselves—all different but OK." Of course, our aim is to be warm and loving and kind to each of our children and to meet their different needs—though inevitably there will be times when we don't manage it perfectly. What the recent research on siblings does show is that differences in children's personalities and adjustment develop for many reasons—the way they interact with each other, the impact of chance events, the different relationships and experiences they each have outside the family. What happens between parent and child is only one small slice of a very big pie.

The thing to remember is that even as toddlers and preschoolers your children are pretty sensitive to inequities or favoritism in the way you treat each of them. Your goal should be to show your appreciation of what is special about each: Appreciation of the uniqueness (to the extent we can possibly manage it) is more likely to help them than preferential treatment.

Chapter 11

ONE PLUS TWO MAKES THREE: TWINS AND SIBLINGS

Learning that you are expecting twins can be a moment for elation—or despair! For some mothers it is a wonderful, unexpected bonus, for others it can feel like a daunting extra load ahead. Your first reaction may be concern for your first child, along the lines of "Oh, how will she take it—one new sibling is bad enough—but *two*!" This chapter covers the changes your family goes through when you have twins after your firstborn child: how firstborn children cope with twin siblings, and how their parents can manage a family that shoots from three members to five.

A TWIN PREGNANCY

Take Care of Yourself

A twin pregnancy puts an extra strain on you physically, so it's especially important to take care of yourself, even more so when you already have a toddler or young child to look after. Rest for you is in *everybody's* best interest: Your twins will be given the best chance and you'll be in better shape after the delivery to look after everyone. You'll feel all the fatigue and strain we've discussed earlier in the book for a normal pregnancy, but *more* so. So if you are pregnant with more than one baby you need to pay even *more* attention to the advice offered for a singleton pregnancy—rest, eating properly, trying to keep fit, being careful about not straining your back when picking up your toddler.

On top of the exhaustion, you may have additional anxieties about how you are going to cope with two infants at the same time. It can be a real help to talk to other mothers who have gone through it all, and you could contact a Mothers of Twins Club. It is very natural too, and common, to be concerned about how your twins are developing. Lots of mothers who are expecting twins are convinced there's something wrong with the babies right up to the delivery. It is good to talk about those worries, if you have them, with your doctor. Doctors don't always realize how their offhand comments can alarm mothers: After examining me in the last stages of pregnancy with my twins, one doctor turned to the nurse and asked her to bring the X rays

---

*Note: There are several excellent books on twins, which detail what you can expect in pregnancy, explain the differences between identical and fraternal twins, suggest ways you can manage feeding and caring for the twins in the early weeks, and so on. These are listed at the end of the book. Especially recommended is *The Parents' Guide to Raising Twins* by Elizabeth Friedrich and Cherry Rowland.

taken at the last visit, saying, "I can feel a multiplicity of limbs, but only one head." My reaction was not a calm one!

Preparing Your Firstborn

Of course it is going to be hard for a toddler or preschooler when two babies invade his home and his parents are desperately busy with them. All the points made about preparing your first child in Chapter Two apply here, and even more strongly. Find a book about twins to show him, to explain that there will be two babies appearing in the house.

Most important of all, *enjoy* these last weeks with your first child, in the lull before the storm breaks over everyone.

AFTER THE TWINS' ARRIVAL: THE FIRST FEW MONTHS

Again, the keys to surviving the first months are getting rest for you, enlisting help with the childcare and housework, paying as much attention to your firstborn as possible, and maintaining some semblance of a routine.

When you go home, you may have to leave one or both babies behind in the hospital if they are very small. If so, try to take that as a time to enjoy being with your first child, and concentrate on getting well and strong yourself. Of course, you may well find that your first child has some problems adjusting after the babies come home—but as with the arrival of a single sibling, you will find that the sleeping problems, disrupted toilet training, and endless demands for your attention and help probably will not continue at this pitch for more than a few weeks. It is encouraging that many mothers who bring twins home find that their first child is not as upset as they had feared. Some even think that having two siblings at once means the first child directs less hostility toward the new babies. As Shelley, mother of two-year-old Katya commented: "Katya never showed any hostility to either of them—from the start. She was upset at all the upheaval, I think, but she treated the babies as a pair—and never showed crossness at *them*."

Yet it is bound to be tough on first children, and all the points made earlier about how to minimize the stress on them apply especially strongly now, in the first weeks home.

On help: Don't feel ashamed if you continue to need some help for a long time. The physical demands will diminish, but the emotional demands of dealing with the needs of three children go on for several years.

On routine: All mothers who have looked after twins and another child stress how essential routine is in getting comfortably through the days and nights in the first weeks. As Shelley, mother of two-year-old Katya and one-month-old twins, commented, "It's not having the twins that's hard, so much as having the twins *and* my two-year-old. Routine is what saves me."

Each parent devises a different solution to the difficult equation of how to fit in feeding, naps, changing two babies, *and* finding time for playing with and caring for the first child. Some feed one twin at a time so they can at the same time do things with their older child; others push their twins into a routine of being fed simultaneously—by making one wait if she wakes before the other, by putting them to nap at the same time—so that their older child can have some time *without* the babies around. Each family has to find the pattern that suits it best; the important thing is to be sure that your first child gets some special attention in the mêlée—and doesn't get left to muddle along unhappily on his own. There'll be times when you feel it is hopelessly difficult to find time for everyone, but at least establishing a routine *does* get easier, quite quickly, after the first two to three weeks.

Talk to mothers of twins and you'll get lots of hints about cutting down on the time taken for routine care, and you'll feel reassured about not bathing them so often, about feeding them both from the same cup—and so on. If you don't know anyone who has twins, contact the Mothers of Twins Clubs. The address is given in the appendix.

CRYING

Crying from twin babies can be the last straw for weary parents. It can be pretty hard on firstborn children too. Comforters, pacifiers, thumbs, special cloths, can help everybody. Most books don't encourage you to use pacifiers; however, if you remember the following, there are no grounds for concern. If the pacifier gets dirty, sterilize it by boiling and make sure *never* to hang it around a baby's neck on a ribbon. If you attach the pacifier to a very short ribbon and pin it to the child's clothes, there's no danger of it getting caught around his neck. Most mothers of twins find them a great help. And they are discarded well before thumbs!

If the crying gets too bad, go to bed yourself, and take them with you, lying them on your tummy and chest; doubtless you'll have to have your toddler in bed too—but if even one of them stops crying, that'll help.

If you are at the breaking point, here's what Elizabeth Friedrich and Cherry Rowland recommend in their sensible book *The Parents' Guide to Raising Twins*:

If your twins cry a lot in the early days, do take advantage of any offer of help. Remember the crying affects you much more than it will another person.

If there is no one around to take them off your hands—and this is more than likely in a crisis—then take yourself out. Shut the door on them, turn up the radio to drown them out, make yourself a cup of tea or coffee, take a few deep breaths, and let go of the tension. It need not be for long. With a bit of luck, one or both might have dropped off to sleep in your absence. If not, you can make a fresh start.

In general, you may have to be a bit ruthless about not always attending to the babies' crying as long as nothing serious is wrong.

TIME FOR EACH TWIN

All parents of twins feel that they don't have time for each twin as an individual. This is likely to be especially acute if you also have a toddler or preschooler to look after. You have to remember, though, that only firstborn children *ever* get that exclusive attention from parents, yet later-born children thrive anyway! Some parents in fact feel that it can be an advantage for the babies that they don't have a parent fussing over them too much. Twins can benefit if their parents become more relaxed, as their realization of differences between the children decreases their concern about the particulars of their children's behavior. They see that "normal" kids can be very different. And there's no good evidence that twins develop more psychological problems than singletons as they grow up. So don't worry if your twins are getting less of your attention than a single baby. A climate of love and caring is what matters, not the number of minutes spent with parents.

Twins are sometimes a bit behind on starting to talk—and this may be because they spend less time "talking" with their parents—but this again doesn't appear to be linked to any *problems* later.

Some parents try to find a brief time each day for each twin separately—but you don't have to feel regimented about this. If you begin to find that one twin is regularly getting less attention and play—perhaps because he's the placid, quiet one of the family—then you can try to even things out. But you'll find that there are usually phases in how much attention each twin gets, and it evens out over the longer term. If the twins are noticeably behind on beginning to talk, make sure they aren't being left on their own together too much.

As they grow up, there are lots of interesting things for the twins to watch besides their harassed parents—their older sibling for a start; and then when they begin to play with other people there is, of course, almost always that twin around too. So the scarcity of parental attention becomes less of an issue. And older siblings can be great entertainers for their twin siblings from early days: My own twins watched their older sister, fascinated, far more than they watched each other, in the early months.

LOOK AFTER YOURSELF

It is in everyone's interest that you are well and happy in these early months. It is all too easy to put your own needs for rest and proper food (and for being mothered *yourself*) last on the list of priorities. But don't; take those strictures to look after yourself seriously. It's important, too, to keep seeing other people. Don't get isolated, buried in babies day in and day out. Getting out is hard; simply going shopping is often a struggle with two small children, let alone with three. But it is worth trying hard to make some regular arrangement for getting out of the house without all of them—or preferably without any of them.

THE IMPACT ON OLDER FIRSTBORN CHILDREN

Most three- to five-year-olds and older children cope pretty well with the arrival of twin siblings, and can be a great help to their overwhelmed parents. The issues of organizing a routine and feeding schedules are not as difficult as when you have a toddler and twins, and taking all three out is not such a major feat. For some older firstborns, however, problems arise when the twins reach toddlerhood.

When the Twins Are Toddlers

Apart from the first month or so at home, perhaps the hardest time both practically and emotionally is the stage when you have twin toddlers *and* an older preschool child. The "terrible twos" has its own special meaning now! And for much of the time it may seem that you have the "terrible threes."

SAFETY ISSUES

Even at home, the hazards seem more than doubled when there are three small people on the go. Keeping an eye on everyone requires superhuman vigilance, and a second sense for detecting those suspicious silences when one or more has discovered some forbidden treasure like the bathroom closet full of medicines, or your sewing box. Playpens don't really seem to solve the problem, most mothers report, though one comments that *she* used to get in the playpen, with the children outside, to read the paper in peace! If you can manage to make a space where they can play safely together—maybe half your living room, during the daytime—it's a great help.

All the usual safety precautions take on extra significance when there are three children roaming around: Stair gates (some that would withstand one toddler give way under the weight of two), window catches, limiting access to knives and dangerous utensils and materials, placing high locks on the doors, childproofing the refrigerator door, and so on, all have to be thought about with extra care and attention. Amazingly early you'll find those twins cooperating on dreadful deeds together, sometimes egged on by their older sibling, who wouldn't dream of getting herself into trouble that way, but delights in seeing the evil done. Every family with twins has a series of terrible tales about what the twins did together, starting early in the second year. My neighbor with twins came into the kitchen to find both her twenty-month-old twins had pushed chairs to the cupboard, climbed up, and were, with peals of laughter, systematically taking turns throwing the china plates onto the floor.

PROTECTING YOUR OLDEST

Making sure that your firstborn has time with you continues to be a key issue as the twins get older. You will also probably want to help protect him from the twins' intrusions and depredations as the babies become mobile, charming demons with amazing powers to search-and-destroy. Families manage this in different ways. One strategy is to make sure your firstborn has time with you after the twins have been put to bed at night, as well as during naptimes. One family made Saturday morning a sacred mother-and-oldest-son time, with trips to the shops and library, while Dad looked after the twins. Just remember how little chance a singleton stands in competing for attention with a charming pair of twins, each of whom has developed an irresistible way to claim your attention.

Protecting your firstborn's privacy is key, too, especially if he's a preschooler or older, with his own elaborate games and pursuits. Make sure he has a space that's out of their reach—ideally a room of his own.

An issue that may seem trivial but which often seriously bothers firstborns is the endless attention that baby and toddler twins get from passersby and neighbors as well as relatives. Alison and Joe, parents of three-year-old Ned, decided to try to leave the twins behind on shopping expeditions and outings whenever they could when they saw how much Ned minded all the oohs and ahhs his twin sisters received. The general lesson here is to try to keep an eye open for what upsets your firstborn, and then to see how you can avoid those situations. Of course, it would be good to make sure your twins also get their share of outings, too, perhaps when your firstborn is at school.

GROWING UP TOGETHER

Who Becomes Close to Whom?

The pattern of relationships between firstborn children and their twin siblings can vary considerably. In some families with twins and an older child, after the first year the older child develops a special relationship with one twin, and is less close to the other. It is uncommon for the twins to "gang up" on their older sibling, though some firstborn children do find their exuberant twin siblings overwhelming. When they become mobile, twins can sometimes dominate, and even frighten their sensitive older siblings. If you notice that happening in your family, you may want to keep an eye open for protection for your older child, and make an extra effort to give him time away from those twins. Between the twins themselves, the relationship tends to vary according to whether the twins are identical or fraternal, and according to their gender. Identical twins tend to be closer than fraternal twins, and same-sex fraternal twins closer than boy-girl fraternal twins. But for most families, there's a lot of companionable play among all three children from the second year on—as well as that competitiveness and conflict that can be so tiresome for parents.

COMPETITIVENESS AND CONFLICT

Competitiveness and possessiveness can be particularly acute in a family with twins and another child, not just in the two-year-old phase in which *mine* dominates everything, but throughout childhood to the teenage years and beyond. Wayne, a father with twins and an older boy, now all adolescents, comments that "as teenagers they *still* watch like hawks to see if they're getting fair shares at dinner—and to be sure one of the others isn't being favored."

This competitiveness doesn't mean that they don't also get great strength, comfort, and pleasure from each other's company. Families of three and four children sometimes become particularly close and continue to be so through adolescence when other siblings often drift apart. With these larger families a camaraderie can develop that's a real source of support. But the competitiveness does mean that those strategies for minimizing conflict that were described in Chapters Seven and Eight become particularly important:

- Avoid, like the plague, comparisons between your children—whether explicit or implicit.
- Focus on each child as an individual.
- Praise the nice things they do for each other.
- Put those competitive, hurtful remarks that you overhear them make to each other in the context of the entire relationship.

YOUR OWN NEEDS AND FEELINGS

There may well be moments when, surrounded by wailing children, dirty laundry, a chaotic house, a snappy, irritable spouse, and exhausted by another bad night, you feel a failure as a parent. *All* parents feel this way sometimes, and parents of twins are particularly likely to be pushed to their limits. It is entirely reasonable to feel despair occasionally, and your bouts of misery certainly do *not* mean that you are an inadequate parent. If you can get in touch with other mothers in similar predicaments with whom you can share the horrors and laugh about your plight, that's probably the best tonic. You may also get some hints about getting more of a child-care and household routine which could help. If a sleepless toddler or preschooler is adding to the trouble, try those techniques described earlier (page 174), or ask your doctor for help. If *you* are exhausted from lack of sleep, see if you can get someone to take over for a couple of nights, and go and sleep at a friend's house.

You may also have moments when you feel resentful at the double burden of twins—resentful about what the twins have done to your life and to your relationship with your older child. Talk to other parents of twins, and you'll see how common this cycle of martyrdom and anger followed by guilt can be. Just

talking about the feelings with others who have been through it
will help.

MOTHERS AND FATHERS

It's especially important, too, to find time for you and your spouse
to be together without the children—and not to let those three
demanding children absorb all your time and emotional energy.
Twins do take a toll—let alone twins plus a third, and a house-
ful of three young children often puts stresses on a couple's marriage and sex life. It is another reason to try to get as much help
as you can.

How then can you minimize the stresses on you both as
parents?

· Put your needs as a couple high on the priority list.
· Make sure the kids go to bed at a reasonably early hour, even
  if they don't go to sleep.
· Try to get an occasional night away from the house together.
· Talk about problems with your sex life together.

THE PLEASURES OF HAVING THREE

It is not all problems, of course, with three young children close
together in age. Three special benefits of having children so close
together come immediately to mind:

First, fathers and their children are often closer in families
with twins—the fathers become involved early on whether or
not they intended to, and that closeness in the first year or two
continues.

Second, twins and their older siblings begin to entertain each other remarkably early—and in the second year your twins will probably be a continuing source of interest and games for each other. They'll fight and argue, too, but you're much less likely to have children moping around with nothing to do, bored and unfocused, than are families with only one or even two children.

And third, families with twins and a singly born sibling form a supportive network that can be of great strength. At all the major transition points in their lives, like starting school, moving to a new neighborhood and school, or at times of family crises, the children are likely to close ranks and be supportive of each other. It is not surprising, then, that children with twin siblings commonly say that they *like* having twins in the family, and that they get along well with them. And once the children hit school age, having twins in the family seems to be a real attraction in the eyes of their friends.

SUMMARY OF STRATEGIES FOR FAMILIES WITH TWINS FOR TODDLERHOOD AND BEYOND

- *Give each child some time alone with you.*
  Take any chance—and make chances—to take each child out with you without the others.
- *Welcome their ties with other people.*
  Feel pleased, not jealous, if any one of your children forms a strong relationship with some other adult—whether father, grandparent, or someone else.
- *Care for yourself.*
  Look after yourself so you still have the strength to see the funny side of the daily dramas and disasters.

- *Keep to a schedule.*
Stick to routines of daily care.
- *Stick to your ground rules.*
Keep rules to a minimum, but stick to those you care most about sharing (no violence, etc.) as far as humanly possible and apply them scrupulously fairly to everyone.
- *Avoid comparisons.*
Watch out for comparisons and favoritism. They'll "see" favoritism toward the others however fair you actually are, but at least you can try to minimize it.
- *Give yourself a break.*
Take breaks from everyone, away from the house and the chaos!

Chapter 12

A LOOK AHEAD

Your four-year-old is screaming in despair as your toddler tips over her painting water; it is the fourth battle scene of the afternoon. Wails from the toddler boost the cacophony to an even higher frequency. You've been wiping noses all day, and carrying on at least two—sometimes three—simultaneous conversations. You haven't had five minutes of purely private, adult pleasure for days. When will things get better? Will things get easier? Definitely yes, and quite shortly (unless, glutton for punishment, you embark on a third baby!).

In purely physical terms, the first two years of having two children are unbelievably tiring, hard work, especially if your two are close in age. If you've had twins, of course, then the physical labor has probably been almost beyond endurance. In the following years there'll be endless sibling squabbles and bickering, but not that slogging hard labor which, coupled with interrupted nights, is enough to wear down the most angelic parent. As your second child reaches the third and fourth years, it gets easier to arrange to be away, easier to leave them for work, easier to work at home. You'll even get a few brief glimpses of what adult life used to be like (but let's face it, that child-free adult life will never return). The four-way tug-of-war—with the two children, spouse, and job all pulling in different directions—that seems so impossible to manage now does get easier to deal with as your children get beyond the two-year-old stage. Of course, as the pressures at home relax a bit, you may well choose to take on more work, a full-time job, go back to being a student, have a third baby—and then that vision of a quieter, saner life will recede once again.

In the pages below, I'll take a look at what lies in store for you and your children as they develop through the years of childhood.

WILL THEY FIGHT LESS?

They will fight physically less frequently, yes. However, many six- to ten-year-old siblings, and even teenagers too, keep up the kicking, punching, and slapping. Don't assume that yours are the only school-aged kids who resort to physical aggression.

Arguing will continue for a long while. The real drop in quarreling is often not seen until beyond ten years or so. The balance of power often shifts as the two of them get older. Second siblings who had a tough time winning arguments when they were younger discover new skills at teasing and tormenting their older siblings as they hit five, six, and seven. As one father said of his newly assertive five-year-old: "The worm has definitely turned."

DO QUARRELSOME SIBLINGS EVER GET TO BE FRIENDS?

Many siblings who fight a lot in the first two to three years *do* become friends, if being friends means playing great games together, amusing each other, sharing a sense of humor, and supporting each other in times of stress. Often brothers and sisters start to spend a lot more time playing together when the second child reaches four; a four-year-old can be a real companion for a five-, six-, or seven-year-old. But this doesn't mean they won't go on arguing too. Often the brothers and sisters who fight a lot are the *same kids* who play great games together and share uproarious jokes.

Very often when brothers and sisters reach ten, eleven, and twelve their relationship becomes more distant. Both are leading full lives with friends beyond the family and thus they don't spend as much time with each other; when this happens, that intense intimacy they shared as young children wanes. But the differences between pairs of siblings in this regard are *huge*. Some continue to be close companions throughout adolescence; others drift away from one another as teenagers, then enjoy each other more as young adults.

WHAT HAPPENS TO THEIR RELATIONSHIP
WHEN ONE STARTS SCHOOL?

How much of an upheaval the beginning of school entails depends, in part, on whether a child is used to being away from home, for example, in daycare; much also depends on how things go in school. If your firstborn is unhappy at school or having a hard time adjusting, his unhappiness may well show up most at home in hostility to his younger sibling. Sometimes, however, the sibling left at home wants special attention, and shows new insecurities and jealousies. Second-born children sometimes feel the older one gets all the parental attention *before* and *after* school— and they also envy the treats and excitements they see the sibling getting at school.

When second-born children start school, their older siblings are often a real help. Miranda noted that when Greg, her rather anxious second-born, started school, his supportive older sister "really looked out for him. They used to walk around at recess hand in hand. I'm *sure* it made starting school easier for him—he was worried about it before."

This can be a time when their relationship changes quite a bit. Some brothers and sisters become friendlier when they don't have to spend so much time on top of each other. Others are sad at losing their closeness. The kind of friendships they form at school can contribute to changes in their relationships at home. For example, boys who get to be part of an "all-boys" group and a "boys-only" environment at school often lose interest in their younger sisters. Their sisters often take this hard, and you may need to step in to supply other distractions and entertainment for a while. Ten-year-old Lynne was more philosophical about the change in her relationship with her brother:

"When we were little we were like good friends—not just brother and sister but *really* good friends. Then when we both went to school, that really ended. It's not that we moved apart, it was more that we had new friends, and *different* friends."

WHAT HAPPENS IF A THIRD CHILD IS BORN?

By and large, there's much less upset when a third child is born than there was with the second child's arrival. No one feels quite so displaced as the firstborn did when that usurping second child arrived on the scene. But individual differences in how children respond are striking. Some first and second children get terribly upset and jealous. Others love having a baby around. Siblings who fight constantly with each other are often both loving toward the new baby. If they're very competitive it can also be a new source of competition between them; they'll argue about who gets to take care of the third sibling.

In fact, parents who have three or four children are often quite surprised at the shifting alliances and configurations. One pair may fight all the time with each other but get along splendidly with the other children. Jon noticed this happening with his three children: "Well, Jay, who's in the middle, gets on fine with Lizzie—the youngest—but he's at it hammer and tongs with his older brother Aaron from morning till night. They just seem to know how to needle each other, and they won't let it alone. Yet Aaron and Lizzie do well together too."

As parents of more than two children notice, there are special experiences for children with *both* older and younger siblings. One of the real advantages of having a sibling is that in contrast to playing with a kid of your own age, there is the opportunity of playing either protectively and dominatingly (if you're an older sibling), or as a follower (if you're a younger sibling). If you have both older and younger siblings, you get the chance to experience both.

THE IMPACT OF DIVORCE OR SEPARATION

Following divorce or separation of their parents, some sibling pairs close ranks and provide a very real support for one another. Children who have a close relationship with a sibling are less likely to suffer from emotional problems after a divorce than those who don't have a supportive sibling relationship—as a study by Jenny Jenkins and Marjorie Smith in England showed. Brothers and sisters can, it seems, protect one another in a very real way from some of the stress of family breakup. Many children confide in their *siblings* rather than their friends about their concerns and worries following divorce.

In other families, however, the stress of the divorce results in *more* sibling arguing. In fact, those brothers and sisters who didn't get along too well before the divorce often increase the most in quarrelsomeness after divorce. Usually this is a short-term increase, and when a calmer and more regular pattern of family life is reestablished, the quarrels subside in the majority of families studied. The introduction of stepparents, too, sometimes means a sharp increase in conflict between brothers and sisters. This is especially true in families in which mothers have been alone with their children for a year or more and a special closeness has developed. A stepfather seems like a real interloper to the kids. Girls who have become very close to their mothers seem to have the most trouble when a stepfather joins the family; these girls often show their vulnerability in conflicts with their siblings.

What can parents and stepparents do to minimize the fighting? The same advice that I have emphasized throughout this book applies here—indeed it seems that in families under the stress of divorce and remarriage, siblings become upset for the same reasons as in other families, only the effects are more marked. For example, if children feel that there is favoritism following divorce, the sibling quarrels are *particularly* acute; if you are in a "stepparenting" family, it is especially important to watch out for preferential treatment.

IN THE LONGER TERM ...

Siblings tend to go their own ways increasingly in adolescence, and then, as adults, inevitably their lives take separate courses. But the tie between them is often a very strong one, and when they reach later life they very often become very close again. If you talk to people in their seventies and eighties, most speak of feeling quite *close* to their siblings. And they feel that it is those early years of childhood spent together—the fights, arguments, shared games—that makes them close as older adults. The sibling arguments which seem so fraught with animosity as you deal with them now will be a source of shared amusement and affection to your children when they look back on them years hence. Sisters, for reasons that are not entirely understood but which may have to do with women's greater capacity for emotional involvement with the family, seem especially to hold the key to that mutual closeness and support in later life. So in weathering the storms of siblinghood now, you are helping to foster a relationship that is likely to be a key resource for your children as adults.

CHILDREN'S VIEWS

Finally we'll let some young children who have helped us with our studies of siblings speak for themselves about their relationships with their sisters and brothers. Their remarks highlight how rich and how varied the relationship is between siblings—the friendship, support, teasing and aggression, the sensitivity to favoritism, the understanding they have for one another—all the issues you see in your own children's interaction day in and day out. The siblings speaking here are between six and ten years old:

Mixed feelings

Can you think of a single child who doesn't have ambivalent feelings about her brothers and sisters?

> Well, I love her in a way, because she's my sister—but I don't *like* her much of the time. Sometimes we're friends and sometimes we fight. She annoys me—but I tease her! But she's very nice to me too!
>
> PAUL, YOUNGER SIB, 7 YEARS

> Sometimes I like him and sometimes I don't, because I definitely *hate* him sometimes.
>
> ROSY, OLDER SIB, 10 YEARS

> She's a bit of a pest sometimes but she can be really nice. We can sometimes really have arguments, and sometimes we can be best friends and want to really play together and then sometimes she's very *very* nice!
>
> MOLLY, OLDER SIB, 10 YEARS

Good companions

Almost all siblings describe the pleasure of *playing* with each other, not just during the preschool years, but as they grow up together:

> We really have lots of fun together at night; we talk. We're going to get a mirror in our room so that we can look at each other and see if we were awake or not—so we wouldn't wake the other one up for talking.
>
> DICK, YOUNGER SIB, 6 YEARS

Younger siblings often commented on the inventiveness of older siblings and the excitement of playing with them:

> He's nice to me and we play lots of games together. He likes inventing. I *really* like him when he invents stuff . . . and he plays airplanes with me and that's my favorite game.
>
> JUSTIN, YOUNGER SIB, 6 YEARS

> Her games are *great*! She thinks of so many things for us to do. I like our special games together.
>
> FAY, YOUNGER SIB, AGED 8 YEARS

And older siblings too sometimes comment on what they have learned from their younger siblings. Things parents often don't notice are seen as important:

> She teaches me to skip and she always plays football with me if my friends can't.
>
> DEREK, OLDER SIB, 8 YEARS

Control

But the conflict between siblings also comes up a great deal. Younger siblings often complain of the bossiness and control of older siblings:

> It always has to be his way in a game and not my way. It can *never* be my way. He deliberately comes and annoys me when I want to be alone.
>
> CHRISTY, YOUNGER SIB, 6 YEARS

> She's bossy bossy bossy! Makes me do whatever she wants— gets to choose what we play, says who is to be what in our game.
>
> WALLY, YOUNGER SIB, 8 YEARS

Dislike

Although it is upsetting for parents to recognize, children sometimes describe out-and-out dislike of a sibling:

> She's nasty. And she fights me. And she teases me. She always ticks me off if I go near her.
>
> POLLY, YOUNGER SIB, 6 YEARS

> He's so rough, and horrid to me. I just hate him. I wish he wasn't in our family.
>
> CAITLIN, OLDER SIB, 7 YEARS

Fights

Physical fights are remembered with vividness, and resentment. Children can give you detailed blow-by-blow accounts of their disputes. And they are well aware of how they themselves often precipitate fights:

> All I have to do is say something. It might be nice or hor-
> rible and he just goes and hits me or kicks me. All I have
> to do is say something when he's feeling a bit horrible and
> he hits us all!
>
> CORINNA, OLDER SIB, 7 YEARS

And Reconciliations

But the same siblings who talk about fights also often talk about
the friendly side of their relationship:

> I remember punchups because he kind of says "no! NO!
> That's not fair!" And he hits me and I say "Olly, you
> shouldn't hit!" so he hits me again and I hit him, then he
> hits me and kicks me and tries to do karate on me. I jump
> in the air and he misses and then I kick him! But sometimes
> though he can be friendly like when I was ill last night he
> ran upstairs and got me a blanket and brought it down and
> then he . . . he got all his cuddly toys and shoved them
> under the blanket. Well, he was *trying* to be kind! And then
> he got Ben [dog] and made Ben get on top of me to keep
> me company!
>
> FRANCES, OLDER SIB, 8 YEARS

Older siblings as leaders

Older siblings often report enjoying their leadership role. They
also enjoy seeing their younger siblings choose them as "models"
for their own behavior. Clearly those imitations don't pass
unnoticed!

> Sometimes I like her because she really is rather babyish and
> I like pretending she is my little baby and I like comforting
> her when she cries.
>
> CHERYL, OLDER SIB, 10 YEARS

I like her because I can tell her what to do. I can boss her about a bit.

CRAIG, OLDER SIB, 8 YEARS

I like the way she tries to copy off me sometimes. Yeah, I like that.

KIRSTEN, OLDER SIB, 8 YEARS

Understanding Each Other

Brothers and sisters often know each other well, and sometimes comment in a sophisticated way about why their siblings behave the way they do. Their comments reveal to us how much children can learn about other people—and themselves—from their relationships with their siblings:

When we do argue I think he really isn't angry with me, but he wants to have more control over me really. 'Cos he thinks he's the youngest so we all boss him around, so he annoys me, and that's his way to show his power over me.

FRANCES, OLDER SIB, 8 YEARS

He's a bad loser—and I am too!

DUNCAN, OLDER SIB, 8 YEARS

She doesn't really *mean it* when she gets at me—it's just . . . Kay and I really do know how to annoy each other!

RANDY, YOUNGER SIB, 6 YEARS

We're closer now than we were. Less fights. Basically we know each other's feelings more now.

ZARA, OLDER SIB, 9 YEARS

Jealousy and Favoritism

But jealousy continues, for both older and younger siblings, as children grow up together. For some kids it goes right on into adolescence. It's important for the rest of the family to realize this:

> I'm jealous of her quite a bit—of things that she does, as well as when she's with Mom and Dad.
>
> POLLY, YOUNGER SIB, 10 YEARS

> They always take her sides, do things with her.
>
> RORY, OLDER SIB, 7 YEARS

> I mind a *lot* that she seems to do things with them (our parents) so much more than me.
>
> PAUL, YOUNGER SIB, 7 YEARS

Comparisons

Siblings continually compare themselves with each other.

> Well, I sort of don't like him because he can stack blocks higher than me.
>
> JOHN, YOUNGER SIB, 6 YEARS

> He always tries to boast and climb highest in the tree.
>
> FRANCES, OLDER SIB, 8 YEARS

> She's better at swimming than me—she's on the team. And she can run so fast—faster than me by far. But I'm a better dancer.
>
> MOLLY, OLDER SIB, 10 YEARS

Sometimes they show a surprising degree of self-awareness—and even self-deprecation. Their sensitivity to these comparisons reminds us how powerful an influence a sibling can be on a child's developing sense of self:

> It's normally my fault. I'm the naughtiest one.
>
> PETER, OLDER SIB, 8 YEARS

> He's the clever one. Not me.
>
> GINNY, OLDER SIB, 12 YEARS

Seeing the Differences

Brothers and sisters are very aware of the differences in their personalities and in what they like doing:

> I like playing adventure games and reading books. Oh, no! *She'd* rather play princesses and get out the dressing-up stuff. She does like different things than me.
>
> JEAN, OLDER SIB, 7 YEARS

> We're just *totally* different. He likes doing different things— computer games and things like that—and we have different friends. If he wasn't my brother, I'd never play with him.
>
> ALICE, OLDER SIB, 9 YEARS

Again, it is often clear that their view of *themselves* is closely bound up with how they compare themselves to this other child—whether favorably or unfavorably.

Support and comfort

Siblings are sometimes a real source of comfort for young children and a support in times of trouble. Parents sometimes fail to notice how brothers and sisters help each other in frightening or stressful moments:

I don't like her to be asleep when I'm awake because I get frightened in my bed. It's the most frightening time of the day. 'Cos without her I've got no one to talk to. And no one to see if I was there.

MARK, YOUNGER SIB, 6 YEARS

Comfort offered during illnesses or after accidents is greatly appreciated and long remembered:

When I feel sick, he's always kind to me. . . . He's always kind and brings me presents.

CLARA, OLDER SIB, 9 YEARS

A Relationship That Changes

As the children grow up the relationship can become closer, or more contentious and difficult:

Well, we *used* to be really close, real friends. Then he went to a different school and got into a kind of gang of boys— and now he doesn't want to do things with me. *I'd* like to, but not him.

JESSIE, YOUNGER SIB, 7 YEARS

We used to fight so much . . . over everything. Now it's easier. I think I don't tease her so much, and she doesn't get so upset, and we do things together quite a lot. She's more fun for me now. We like doing lots of the same things now.

ANYA, OLDER SIB, 9 YEARS

Good Friends

For so many sisters and brothers, the last word is the affection they feel, and the *friendship* that they share with their siblings. It is moving and reassuring for us as parents to hear our children talk about the power of that friendship, and the pleasure they find with each other. We'll end with the comments of three who had no doubts about their liking for their siblings:

> Well, I just like him. I like him in a lot of ways. I like him especially because he's my brother. I like him very much. . . . I just think he's very nice—he's cute!
>
> ZARA, OLDER SIB, 9 YEARS

> Can't think of anything I don't like about her!
>
> DEREK, OLDER SIB, 8 YEARS

> He's a good friend—the best!
>
> JASON, YOUNGER SIB, 6 YEARS

Appendix

HELPFUL ORGANIZATIONS

For Parents of Twins:

Mothers of Twins Clubs
There are local clubs for parents of twins located throughout the country. To find one in your area, check your local telephone directory or ask your doctor. Or contact the National Organization of Mothers of Twins Clubs, Inc., 5402 Amberwood Lane, Rockville, MD 20853.

Center for Study of Multiple Birth
339 East Superior Street, Chicago, IL 60611. Telephone: (312) 266-9093. Will provide a list of publications on request.

Double Talk
Box 412, Amelia, OH 45102. A newsletter for parents of twins.

Twinline
P.O. Box 10066, Berkeley, CA 94709. Telephone: (415) 644-0861. Advice by phone or leaflets and reading list of useful publications.

Other Helpful Organizations:

Le Leche League International

9616 Minneapolis Avenue, Franklin Park, IL 60131. Telephone: (312) 455-7730. Call or write for the address and number of your local La Leche League. Provides support and encouragement for nursing mothers, through local volunteers.

Nursing Mothers Counsel, Inc.

P.O. Box 500063, Palo Alto, CA 94303. Help on nursing.

Parents Anonymous

6733 South Sepulveda Boulevard, Suite 270, Los Angeles, CA 90045. Telephone: (800) 421-0353 in all states except California; in California (800) 352-0386. Provides help for parents under stress.

Parents of Premature and High-Risk Infants International, Inc.

c/o National Self-Help Clearinghouse, 24 West 43 Street, Room 620, New York, NY 10036. Telephone: (212) 642-2944. A source of information, referrals, and support for those with infants who require special care.

Bibliography

L. B. Ames and C. C. Haber. *He Hit Me First: When Brothers and Sisters Fight* (New York: Warner Books, 1982).

R. Ferber. *Solve Your Child's Sleep Problems* (New York: Simon and Schuster, 1985).

E. Friedrich and C. Rowland. *The Parents' Guide to Raising Twins* (New York: St. Martin's Press, 1984).

H. G. Ginott. *Between Parent and Child* (New York: Avon Books, 1969).

A. Hochschild. *The Second Shift* (New York: Avon Books, 1989).

Index

adolescents, 189–90
  in becoming friends, 186
  fighting and, 185
  rivalries and, 127
  twins and, 179
aggression, 4–5
  fighting and, 130
  in first year of living together,
    97–100
  homecomings and, 69, 76
  outside of family, 133
  see also hitting and hurting
ambivalence, 14, 117–19, 191
Ames, Louise Bates, 131, 147
anger, 126
  and caring for two, 17, 22,
    24–25
  fighting and, 131
  in first year of living together,
    99–102
  and hitting and hurting,
    150–53
  homecomings and, 69
  hospital stays and, 53–54, 58
  and preparing for new arrivals,
    35, 42
  twins and, 180
anxieties, 187
  conflict and, 137
  in first year of living together,
    95–97

homecomings and, 61, 81
hospital stays and, 54
and preparing for new arrivals,
  37, 40–41
rivalries and, 127
sibling differences and, 166
twins and, 170
apologies, 154
arguing, *see* quarrels
attention, *see* love and
  attention

baby-sitters, 43, 80
  in first year of living together,
    85, 89, 103–4, 106
bathing, 47
  in first year of living together,
    86, 95–96, 98, 102,
    104–5, 108–9
  homecomings and, 62, 72–73,
    75, 79–80
  twins and, 173
bedtime, *see* sleeping
Between Parent and Child (Ginott),
  155
birth order, 166–67
births, having firstborns present at,
  55–56

caring for two, 9–25
  changes in, 9, 13–16

Acknowledgments

In this book I have drawn on the comments and insights of many parents and children. Those I have interviewed and talked with in my studies of siblings gave generously of their time. My special thanks to them all, for their help, their wisdom, and their good humor! The research was supported by grants from the Medical Research Council of Great Britain and the National Institute of Health in the United States. My thanks, too, to Carla Glasser, who first suggested a book on surviving the first years of having two children, and who was always encouraging and enthusiastic, and to Ginny Faber for her many thoughtful and sensible editorial suggestions—and her own insights as a mother of two.

About the Author

JUDY DUNN is Distinguished Professor of Human Development at the Pennsylvania State University and the recent recipient of a Guggenheim Fellowship. An international authority on childhood development, she has carried out research on children's development at the Medical Research Council Unit at the University of Cambridge in England, where she was also a Fellow of King's College. She has pioneered research on children's sibling relationships and the use of naturalistic observations to study children's understanding and emotional development. She has conducted several longitudinal studies of children in both the United States and in Great Britain. Her previous books include *Siblings: Love, Envy, and Understanding* (1982), *The Beginnings of Social Understanding* (1988), *Young Children's Close Relationships* (1993), and with Robert Plomin, *Separate Lives* (1990). She is the mother of three children and two stepchildren and lives in the United States and in England.